Vegetable Dishes

DAVID & CHARLES

Newton Abbot London

British Library Cataloging in Publication Data
Vegetable dishes.—(David & Charles Kitchen Workshop)
  1. Cookery (Vegetables)
  I. Gronnsaker. *English*
  641.6'5   TX801

ISBN 9-7153-8478-3

© Text: David & Charles 1983
  Colour illustrations: A/S Hjemmet 1980
  Line illustrations: A/S Hjemmet 1980

Filmset by MS Filmsetting Limited, Frome, Somerset
and printed in The Netherlands
by Smeets Offset BV, Weert
for David & Charles (Publishers) Limited
Brunel House, Newton Abbot, Devon

Vegetables

Vegetables are tasty. Furthermore, vegetables are an important source of the vitamins and minerals which are such an essential part of our diet. In this book we try to inspire you to use more vegetables, the old faithfuls as well as the more exotic ones.

Facts Worth Knowing:
Buying

When buying vegetables, your motto should invariably be that only the best is good enough, whether you buy them in a greengrocer's, at a market stall or in a supermarket. Preferably buy them when they are in season and at their least expensive. Some vegetables, however, can be bought nearly all the year round at approximately the same price.

Vegetables which have been kept too long will have lost their flavour and goodness. Root vegetables with a lot of earth adhering are also a bad buy as you will lose weight and nourishment when cleaning them. On the other hand, although commercially ready-washed vegetables save work, as a rule they are more expensive and do not keep so well. Frozen vegetables cost more than fresh, but one saves weight loss through preparation – not to mention time, which is important to most of us. As regards flavour and nourishment, they are close to what we get when buying fresh vegetables. Canned vegetables tend to lose flavour, nutritional value and colour, and to be rather bland. But makes vary and some canned peas, for instance, are very good. Also, if the fresh vegetable you need for a particular recipe is out of season and therefore costly, the canned variety will provide a very satisfactory substitute. Canned vegetables have another great advantage, you can keep them almost indefinitely without their taking up valuable fridge or freezer space.

Storage

Fresh vegetables should be stored in a dark, cool place. Small quantities can be placed in the fridge's vegetable drawer. Large quantities of vegetables such as carrots, and beetroot, keep best if stored in moist sand or sawdust. Potatoes should be stored in a dark, cool but frostproof place. Onions can be strung and hung up.

Lettuce and fresh herbs should be rinsed well, excess water shaken off, and placed in plastic bags in the fridge, where they should keep fresh and crisp for up to 5 days.

Tomatoes, apples, pears and plums produce a gas called ethylene which reduces the keeping-time of vegetables. This applies particularly to cucumber, cauliflower, lettuce and herbs. Be careful, therefore, to store these well away from fruit.

Quantity Needed
It is difficult to give a guide – so much depends on individual appetite. Obviously, served on their own as a main course, one must allow more than if served as accompaniment. Don't overload the plate with great heaps of vegetables – smaller portions, perfectly cooked, interesting in colour and attractively arranged, are much more inviting. Remember when buying that weight loss in preparation can amount to as much as 40 per cent for some varieties. Frozen vegetables lose between 5 and 10 per cent in weight through defrosting.

Freezing
This section is aimed at those who wish to freeze their own vegetables, whether home-cultivated or bought in season. To be suitable for the freezer, the vegetables should be freshly picked and of first-rate quality. Clean well and, if necessary, cut into large pieces, cubes, slices or strips. This is especially important for varieties you blanch before freezing.

Blanching
Place cleaned or sliced vegetables in a wire basket and lower this into a

Vegetable	Preparation	Blanching Time
Asparagus	leave untied	3–5 min
Brussels sprouts	leave whole	4–5 min
Cabbage	shred	2 min
Carrots	small whole sliced	5 min 3 min
Cauliflower	divide into sprigs	3 min
Celeriac	slice or cube	2–4 min
Corn-on-the-cob	young whole kernels	5–7 min 3 min
French beans	whole or sliced	3 min
Herbs	chop or as sprigs	none
Kale	chop	2–3 min
Leeks	slice	none
Mixed vegetables	according to type	separately, then mix
Onions	slice	none
Peas	shell	2 min
Peppers	halve, remove seeds, slice	2 min
Spinach	leaves left whole	2 min
Sprouting broccoli	cut lengthways	3 min

NOTE When cooking frozen vegetables, deduct the minutes of blanching time.

large saucepan containing an ample amount of boiling water. Estimate time of blanching (see list on previous page) from the moment the water starts to boil again. Blanching should always be done over strong heat. Lift out basket, plunge into ice-cold water and let vegetables cool for at least 2 min. Change the water several times to make sure it is always cold. Place a generous amount of ice cubes in it if you like. Allow water to drain off vegetables and wrap them ready for the freezer.

A Different Way of Freezing

Place ears of corn, peas, green beans, sprigs of cauliflower and other small vegetables in a single layer on a tray. Cover with plastic or tinfoil and leave in the freezer for a couple of hours. Remove, and put vegetables in trays and bags especially made for freezing – tinfoil trays with lids, freezer bags, plastic bags. Label all packages clearly with both name of vegetable and weight, as well as the date of freezing.

Unsuitable for the Freezer

Aubergines, cucumbers, courgettes, celery, whole tomatoes and potatoes can be frozen, but are not suitable for eating without cooking. Salad greens and radishes cannot be frozen at all.

Ways of Cooking

Boiling

Even when it comes to something as simple as boiling vegetables, certain rules should be followed to obtain the best possible flavour, consistency and colour and to retain as many of the vitamins as possible:

- Always place vegetables (whole or sliced) in boiling water. There should be barely enough to cover them.
- Never boil for longer than necessary, ie until barely tender. We should feel crispness when we chew.
- Always add salt to the water except in the case of potatoes you are going to use for purée or mash. Salt can spoil the creamy consistency.
- Always serve vegetables the moment they are ready. They will deteriorate rapidly if you keep them warm for long.
- The water the vegetables are cooked in (the stock) can be used for soups, sauces or stews.

Steaming

You can steam vegetables on a perforated insert or in a special collapsible metal basket. You can even improvise with a colander inside a saucepan, so long as the lid fits tightly.

Have only a small amount of water in the saucepan – 50–100ml (2–4fl oz) is generally enough. The lid must fit tightly. Cooking time will be about 30 per cent longer than for ordinary boiling. Steamed vegetables retain more of their flavour than when boiled, but the vitamin content will be about the same.

Pressure Cooking

Cooking in a pressure cooker is best

suited to vegetables which take a long time to cook, such as potatoes, celery, whole carrots, beetroot and other root vegetables.

It is very important to follow the instructions that come with the pressure cooker. In a matter of a minute or two you can overcook your vegetables and they will be flavourless and unattractive.

If vegetables requiring different cooking times are to be processed together, those requiring longer cooking can be cut into smaller pieces or cooked for a short time before the others are added.

Serving Freshly Boiled or Steamed Vegetables

Freshly boiled, piping hot vegetables are excellent with all kinds of meat and fish dishes. But they can also be served on their own as a separate course, usually with chilled butter, herb butter or one of the classic sauces. Or try a tasty and nourishing sauce like this one: mix a raw egg yolk with a pinch of salt, a dash of pepper and a generous amount of finely chopped parsley.

Boiled or Steamed Left-overs

Freshly boiled vegetables always have the best flavour, but here is a way of using up left-overs, or a mixture of the two. Sprinkle generously with chopped herbs – to add both flavour and vitamins. Mix together equal portions of butter and flour in a saucepan on low heat. Whisk in vegetable or chicken stock and bring to the boil, stirring all the time. Simmer sauce for at least 5 min. Stir in a little sour cream or cream and season with salt, pepper and spices to taste.

Pour over freshly boiled hot vegetables or mix with cold left-overs. Mix 1–2 egg yolks into the sauce for extra nourishment.

Served au Gratin

Mix grated cheese into the sauce (see last paragraph) before combining it with the vegetables. Or sprinkle grated cheese directly onto the vegetables in an ovenproof dish and heat in the oven at 200–220°C, 400–425°F, Gas 6–7. Place the dish high up in the oven to allow the surface to become golden brown.

Other Ways of Serving

Boiled or steamed vegetables can be used as filling in omelettes, or in soufflés. They can also be placed in marinade and served as a salad, or mixed with raw vegetables in salads.

Fried Vegetables

Most raw vegetables can be fried in a frying pan, but this method is especially suitable for potatoes, tomatoes, onions, aubergines (egg plants), peppers, courgettes and mushrooms. The vegetables should be of equal size and cut into thin sticks, slices or cubes.

Dry the peeled and washed vegetables on paper towels and fry in butter, margarine, oil or lard. Keep an even heat and turn them often to make sure they are golden brown all over and tender inside. Sprinkle with salt and spices or herbs after frying. If you add salt before frying, this may extract moisture and prevent the vegetables from going brown.

Some vegetables also lend themselves to deep-frying in a chip pan, potatoes being the classic example. Make sure the fat or oil is really hot before putting in the vegetables in their basket, so that their outside becomes crisp.

Braising in Butter

Vegetables prepared in this way taste delicious, have a good consistency, and the colour and vitamin content are well preserved.

All kinds of vegetables can be butter braised, from the larger varieties like cauliflower and root vegetables, to small ones like peas, mushrooms and thin beansprouts.

Wash vegetables well. Small vegetables are steamed whole, but vegetables such as carrots, celery and parsnip are chopped or coarsely

grated. Divide cauliflower into sprigs, and cut leeks into rings. Braise in butter with a couple of spoonfuls of salted vegetable stock or water added. Use low heat and put a lid on the saucepan. Cooking doesn't take long. Frozen vegetables are especially suited to this method. Usually they have been blanched before freezing – they have been allowed to boil for a couple of minutes and then quickly cooled – and therefore they need a shorter cooking time. It is not necessary to make a sauce for butter-braised vegetables.

Cooking in the Oven – Potatoes
Potatoes are perfectly suited to being cooked or baked in the oven. Large, whole potatoes can be baked in their jackets. Brush potato well to clean it, rinse, dry and prick with a fork to prevent skin from bursting during cooking. Place potatoes on a grid or in an ovenproof dish in oven preheated to 200°C, 400°F, Gas 6. To make the most of the heat, the potatoes can be baked with a casserole meal, bread or anything else, so long as the temperature suits them all. Cooking time depends on the size of the potatoes, but $1-1\frac{1}{2}$ hr is usually enough.
You can also peel raw potatoes and cook them in the oven – whole, halved, or cut into rounds or wedges. Here are a few suggestions:
● Cut potatoes lengthways, brush cut edges liberally with butter or oil and sprinkle with salt and other spices, such as caraway. Bake potatoes in a roasting tin or ovenproof dish at 200°C, 400°F, Gas 6 for 40–60 min.
● Cut preferably oblong potatoes into thin slices almost all the way through, but making sure they hang together at the bottom. Sprinkle with salt and a few breadcrumbs or

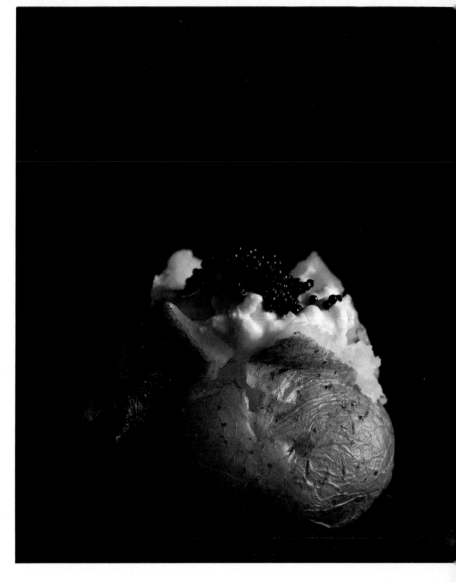

grated cheese. Brush with melted butter and bake in a greased, ovenproof dish at 200°C, 400°F, Gas 6 for 40–60 min.
● If you are serving roast for dinner, cut potatoes in oblong wedges and place in the roasting tin along with meat for the last 20–40 min of cooking time. Add spices if liked. Baste occasionally with the juices from the meat, adding more gravy if necessary.
● Cut potatoes into thin slices and place in a greased ovenproof dish. Sprinkle with spices in between layers and dot butter over top. Add good gravy, stock or cream and bake for 45–60 min at 200°C, 400°F, Gas 6.

A little crushed garlic and onion or leek rings can be placed with the potatoes to vary the flavour.

Other Oven-cooked Vegetables
Hollowed-out and stuffed tomatoes, aubergines, onions, marrows, courgettes and peppers are often baked in the oven. The stuffing is usually minced meat, rice etc. Always add a little liquid to the tin.
Nearly all kinds of vegetables can be sliced and added to meat or fish, then baked in the oven in ovenproof dishes. Vegetables such as tomatoes and cucumber give enough juice when cooking to keep the meat or fish moist, otherwise liquid must be incorporated to prevent it going dry.

Cauliflower

'The cauliflower is the most beautiful of all flowers', was how one gourmet described it, and it is largely true. Certainly few vegetables can surpass it for looks and delicate flavour. It is versatile too, being just as good raw in salads or as a dip vegetable as it is in soups or casseroles, either mixed with other vegetables or on its own. Cauliflower is on the market from late summer right through until about June, though the price varies considerably during that time. Look for a close-packed, creamy white head and remember that the leaves, too, can be used in many recipes.

Cauliflower in Parsley Sauce is very good with ham, mince patties or fried or smoked fish.

To Boil Cauliflower

1 Remove as much of the green leaves as you wish and some of the thick stem. Rinse well and score a cross on the base.

2 Leave cauliflower in cold water with 1 × 5ml tsp (1tsp) vinegar per litre (1¾pt) water for about 1 hr. This will get rid of any insects that may be in it.

3 Place cauliflower in boiling, lightly salted water and allow to boil, covered, for 10–20 min. Don't overboil or it will begin to go mushy.

4 Remove from saucepan with a slotted spoon, drain well and place on a hot serving dish.

Cauliflower with Savoury Rice contains several different vegetables.

Cauliflower in Parsley Sauce
(serves 4)
Preparation time: 10 min
Cooking time: about 30 min
Unsuitable for the freezer

1 large cauliflower
1 × 5ml tsp (1tsp) vinegar per litre
  (1¾pt) water
25g (1oz) butter
1 × 15ml tbsp (1tbsp) flour
cauliflower stock
100–200ml (4–7fl oz) single cream
grated nutmeg
salt, white pepper
sprig of parsley

1 Clean and boil cauliflower as shown in illustrations. Pour some of the cauliflower stock into a bowl and keep cauliflower warm, covered by the saucepan lid, in the remainder.
2 Melt butter in a saucepan, stir in flour and let mixture sizzle for a couple of minutes on low heat without allowing it to brown. Dilute with warm cauliflower stock, a little at a time, until sauce is thick and smooth. Allow to boil for a couple of minutes. Stir in cream and add nutmeg, salt and pepper, and finely chopped parsley.
3 Place cauliflower on a hot serving dish and pour sauce over. Some liquid will always escape from the cauliflower even though it has been well drained, and the sauce must be thick enough to allow for this dilution.
Serve with ham, chops, mince patties, chicken, fried or smoked fish.

Cauliflower with Savoury Rice
(serves 6)
Preparation time: 15 min
Cooking time: about 30 min
Suitable for the freezer, but will lose some flavour

3 small cauliflowers
1 × 5ml tsp (1tsp) vinegar per 1 litre
  (1¾pt) water
salt, pepper
2 onions
40g (1½oz) butter
175g (6oz) long-grain rice
400ml (¾pt) chicken stock

pinch of saffron or ½ × 5ml tsp (½tsp)
  turmeric
2 stalks of celery or 1 slice celeriac
2 leeks
2 × 15ml tbsp (2tbsp) tomato purée
350g (¾lb) cooked ham, cubed
225g (8oz) shelled peas
paprika
finely chopped parsley

1 Place cauliflowers in cold, lightly salted vinegar-water.
2 Sauté roughly chopped onion in 15g (½oz) butter, stir in rice and add all but 2 × 15ml tbsp (2tbsp) warm stock, saffron or turmeric and ½–1 × 5ml tsp (½–1tsp) salt. Boil on low heat for 20 min under a tight-fitting lid.
3 Cook thin leek rings and sliced celery or grated celeriac for 8–10 min in remaining butter and stock. Add tomato purée, ham and peas. Heat through thoroughly.
4 Cook cauliflowers until tender. Stir ham mixture into cooked rice and season with pepper, paprika and salt, if necessary.
Arrange rice and well-drained cauliflowers on a hot serving dish and sprinkle with chopped parsley.
A green salad and bread rolls go well with this dish.

Cauliflower Soufflé

(serves 4)
Preparation time: 20 min
Cooking time: about 1 hr
Oven temperature: 200 and 160°C,
400 and 325°F, Gas 6 and 3
Bottom part of the oven
Uncooked, it is suitable for the
freezer

1 large cauliflower
salt, pepper
50g (2oz) butter
200ml (7fl oz) stock
85g (3½oz) flour
100ml (4fl oz) single cream
4 eggs, separated
breadcrumbs

1 Wash cauliflower, divide into
sprigs and rinse well. Boil until
barely tender in lightly salted water
then drain well, keeping stock.
2 Bring butter and cream to the
boil. Add flour mixed with stock and
stir vigorously until sauce is thick,
shiny and cooked through. Cool a
little.
3 Stir egg yolks into sauce, one at
a time, and season with salt and
pepper. Beat egg whites until peaks
form. Stir 2–3 spoonfuls into sauce,
then carefully fold in remainder.
Mix cauliflower into sauce, stirring
as little as possible.
4 Spoon everything into a greased
ovenproof soufflé dish – it should
not be more than three-quarters
full. Sprinkle surface lightly with
breadcrumbs.
5 Bake for 15 min at 200°C, 400°F,

Gas 6, then reduce heat to 160°C,
325°F, Gas 3 and bake for further
45 min or so. Do not open oven door
for the first 30 min of baking time.
Serve immediately with bread and
butter and a slice of ham.

VARIATION
Place lightly cooked sprigs of cauliflower in a greased dish. Beat 4 eggs
with 400ml (¾pt) milk, about 75g
(3oz) grated cheese, 1 × 5ml tsp
(1tsp) salt, ¼ × 5ml tsp (¼tsp) white
pepper and a pinch of grated
nutmeg.
Pour egg mixture into dish. Butter 2
slices of a sandwich loaf and sprinkle
them with a little more grated
cheese. Place them on top of egg
mixture and bake for 20–30 min at
200–220°C, 400–425°F, Gas 6–7,
depending on the height of the dish.

Cauliflower Polonaise

(serves 4)
Preparation time: 15 min
Cooking time: about 15 min
Unsuitable for the freezer

1 large cauliflower
vinegar, salt, pepper
2 eggs
100g (¼lb) butter
3 × 15ml tbsp (3tbsp) breadcrumbs
3 × 15ml tbsp (3tbsp) parsley

1 Wash and cook cauliflower as
shown in illustrations on pages
10–11.
2 Hardboil the eggs and chop them.
3 Melt butter, stir in breadcrumbs

and sauté lightly. Add chopped
eggs, finely chopped parsley and a
pinch of salt and pepper.
4 Place cauliflower on a hot serving
dish and pour butter mixture over.
Serve warm with smoked mackerel,
ham, pork or chicken.

Cauliflower Soup

(serves 4)
Preparation time: 15 min
Cooking time: about 20 min
Suitable for the freezer, but will lose
some flavour

2 shallots
40g (1½oz) butter
1 cauliflower
1 litre (1¾pt) chicken stock
1 × 15ml tbsp (1tbsp) flour
200ml (7fl oz) single cream
2 egg yolks
salt, pepper, nutmeg
finely chopped parsley

1 Sauté finely chopped shallots in
15g (½oz) butter on low heat. Add
cauliflower sprigs and stock and
simmer until cauliflower is tender.
2 Mix flour with 25g (1oz) softened
butter and stir in. Beat egg yolks
with cream, stir in some of the hot
stock and pour mixture back into
saucepan. Do not allow soup to boil
after this. Season with salt, pepper
and nutmeg. Serve very hot with a
generous sprinkling of parsley and
French bread or toast, and butter.

VARIATION
Follow method 1 of Cauliflower
Soup. Then rub the cooked cauliflower through a sieve, or mash in a
blender. Add back to stock. Reheat
stock, omit flour and butter but
thicken with egg yolks and cream.
Season and serve as before.

Cauliflower in Cheese Sauce

(serves 4)
Preparation time: 15 min
Cooking time: about 15 min
Unsuitable for the freezer

1 large cauliflower
vinegar
salt, pepper, nutmeg
40g (1½oz) butter
1 × 15ml tbsp (1tbsp) flour
200ml (7fl oz) stock
200ml (7fl oz) single cream
75g (3oz) grated cheese
4 thin bacon rashers

1 Wash cauliflower and place in a saucepan of lightly salted boiling water to which 1 × 5ml tsp (1tsp) vinegar per litre (1¾pt) water has been added. When just tender, drain off and retain stock, and keep cauliflower warm under lid.

2 Melt 25g (1oz) butter and stir in flour over low heat. Add cauliflower stock and cream until you have a smooth, not too thick, sauce. Boil for a couple of minutes. Remove from heat, season and stir in 50g (2oz) grated cheese and a little nutmeg.

3 Place well-drained cauliflower in an ovenproof dish, pour cheese sauce over and sprinkle with the remaining grated cheese. Dot top with remaining butter and put dish under a hot grill or in a hot oven until cheese has melted.

4 Fry bacon rashers until crisp, crush and sprinkle over top.

Cauliflower au Gratin

(serves 4)
Preparation time: 15 min
Cooking time: about 30 min
Oven temperature: 240°C, 475°F, Gas 9
Unsuitable for the freezer

1 large cauliflower
salt, pepper
250g (9oz) cooked ham
200g (7oz) boiled spaghetti
300ml (½pt) cheese sauce (see method)

Cauliflower au Gratin is a very tasty everyday dish. The same goes for Cauliflower in Cheese Sauce and Cauliflower Soup (left).

50g (2oz) grated cheese
grated nutmeg
25g (1oz) butter

1 Divide cauliflower into sprigs, wash and boil until nearly tender in lightly salted water.

2 Make up cheese sauce as in previous recipe.

3 Mix cauliflower, chopped ham and spaghetti and put into a greased, ovenproof dish.

Pour cheese sauce over and sprinkle with a little grated nutmeg and the grated cheese. Dot butter over and bake in the oven at 240°C, 475°F, Gas 9 until all is warmed through and golden.

Cabbage

There are many varieties of cabbage which are available, in one form or another, all the year round. The following recipes show that it need not be just a commonplace accompaniment to meat, but can be used in a number of exciting ways.

Spring greens – immature cabbage – are dark green and very good. They are followed by the more mature cabbage in later spring and summer. These in turn are followed by the crinkly leaved savoys of autumn and winter and by the winter varieties.

Stuffed Cabbage

(serves 6)
Preparation time: 25 min
Cooking time: about 1½ hr
Unsuitable for the freezer

1 medium-sized cabbage
250g (9oz) minced beef
250g (9oz) pork, minced
1 onion
salt, pepper, thyme
2 × 15ml tbsp (2tbsp) finely chopped
  parsley
2 × 15ml tbsp (2tbsp) capers
3 × 15ml tbsp (3tbsp) flour
2 eggs
200–300ml (7–10fl oz) milk

1 Wash cabbage, remove any damaged leaves and make a cross on the base. Boil in lightly salted water for

At the back: Stuffed Cabbage. Middle: Cabbage with Ham and Potatoes. Front: Cabbage Patties with fried eggs and stuffed olives.

about 30 min, depending on size – it must still be quite firm.
2 Drain cabbage and carefully hollow out the centre (keep this to use in soups or stews).
3 Mix together the minced meats, grated onion, salt, pepper, thyme to taste, parsley, capers, flour, beaten eggs and milk.
4 Stuff cabbage with meat mixture and place it in a casserole or saucepan with 500ml (1pt) salted water or thin stock. Cover with lid or tinfoil. Simmer on low heat for 40–50 min, or until stuffing is cooked. Pour off meat juices and use in a sauce, soup or stew.
Serve cabbage warm with boiled rice and Tomato Sauce (see page 43).

VARIATION
Make the stuffing with 400g (14oz) minced meat and 100g (¼lb) finely chopped bacon. Proceed as before.

Cabbage with Ham and Potatoes

(serves 6)
Preparation time: 10 min
Cooking time: about 25 min
Unsuitable for the freezer

2 small or 1 large cabbage
salt, white pepper, mustard
50g (2oz) butter
1 × 15ml tbsp (1tbsp) flour
100–200ml (4–7fl oz) single cream
6–8 boiled potatoes
150g (5oz) cooked ham
finely chopped parsley

1 Wash cabbage and cut into four or eight wedges, depending on size. Boil until tender, but not soft, in lightly salted water.
2 Melt half the butter, stir in flour and sauté for a couple of min on low heat. Dilute with boiling stock from cabbage and with cream until it becomes a smooth, not too thick, sauce. Simmer for a couple of min and season with mustard, salt and white pepper.
3 Cut potatoes into slices and the ham into strips and heat in the sauce. Stir in remaining butter. Drain cabbage well and place in a warm ovenproof dish. Pour sauce over and sprinkle with chopped parsley.
Serve hot with bread and more mustard, if necessary.

VARIATION
Meat left-overs can be used with the cabbage, for instance chicken and sausage. Potatoes can be replaced by, for instance, cooked mixed vegetables. Although mustard is the best addition for ham, for chicken and sausage the sauce could be seasoned with paprika, tomato purée or grated cheese.

Cabbage Patties

(serves 4)
Preparation time: 20 min
Cooking time: about 20 min
Suitable for the freezer, but will lose some flavour

1 small cabbage
salt, pepper, paprika
250g (9oz) cooked minced pork
2 large or 3 small eggs
4–5 × 15ml tbsp (4–5tbsp)
  breadcrumbs
butter
flour
6–8 stuffed olives
2 slices cooked ham (optional)

1 Wash cabbage, cut into four and boil for 10 min in lightly salted water. Retain cooking water, but remove cabbage and squeeze out excess water.
2 Stir 1 × 5ml tsp (1tsp) salt into minced pork. Run cabbage once through a mincer and mix into minced pork with eggs, breadcrumbs and seasonings.
3 Shape mixture into flat patties and fry in butter on low heat until golden brown on both sides. Place patties on top of halved ham slices, preheated in a little butter mixed with sliced olives.
4 Deglaze frying pan with cabbage water to make a gravy and season to taste. Thicken with a little flour or cornflour, dissolved in a little cold water.
Serve the patties with fried eggs, boiled potatoes and gravy.

VARIATION
The patties can be made from cabbage only. Instead of minced pork add 3–4 more eggs and enough breadcrumbs to make mixture hold together. These vegetarian cabbage patties can be flavoured with grated onion and a good pinch of dry mustard.

Cabbage Casserole

(serves 4–5)
Preparation time: 10 min
Cooking time: 15–20 min
Browning time: about 10 min at 240°C, 475°F, Gas 9
Unsuitable for the freezer

about 1kg (2¼lb) cabbage
150g (5oz) bacon rashers
salt, pepper, nutmeg, oil
1–2 onions
5 eggs
250ml (9fl oz) milk
2–3 × 15ml tbsp (2–3tbsp) sour
*   cream or cream cheese*

1 Wash cabbage, shred and boil until tender, but not soft, in lightly salted water. Use only 200–300ml (7–10fl oz) water and cook under a tight-fitting lid.
2 Reserve a couple of slices of bacon for garnishing. Snip the rest into small pieces and fry in a little oil until crisp. Place in an ovenproof dish. Fry chopped onion in same fat and mix with bacon.
3 Beat eggs with milk and sour cream or puréed cream cheese and mix with cabbage. Season and add

nutmeg, remembering that bacon itself is salty.
4 Place cabbage on top of bacon. Arrange remaining bacon on top. Place dish in oven as directed until bacon is lightly golden and everything heated through. Serve hot with a tomato salad or other salad.

Sauerkraut

Use either ordinary or red cabbage. Sauerkraut is suitable for the freezer.

1kg (2¼lb) cabbage
1 × 15ml tbsp (1tbsp) flour
2 × 5ml tsp (2tsp) salt
3 × 15ml tbsp (3tbsp) caraway seeds
50ml (2fl oz) water
1–2 × 15ml tbsp (1–2tbsp) vinegar
2 × 15ml tbsp (2tbsp) sugar
25g (1oz) butter

1 Cut cabbage in half, remove the middle stalk and coarse outer leaves, then shred.
2 Place cabbage, flour, salt and caraway seeds in layers in a casserole. Add water and vinegar.
3 Allow cabbage to simmer, covered, for at least 1½ hr, then add sugar. Finally stir in butter.

Cabbage in Cream Sauce

(serves 4)
Preparation time: 15 min
Cooking time: 15–20 min
Suitable for the freezer

½ a large or 1 small cabbage
salt, peppercorns, nutmeg
3 × 15ml tbsp (3tbsp) flour
250ml (9fl oz) single cream
25g (1oz) butter

1 Wash cabbage and cut into pieces. Boil until tender, but not too soft, in lightly salted water containing 6–8 whole peppercorns. Use about 200ml (7fl oz) water and boil under a tight-fitting lid. Drain well, reserving cooking water.
2 Mix flour with a little cold cabbage stock. Stir in cream, bring to the boil then add butter, salt to taste and nutmeg.
3 Add cabbage and heat through. Serve with meat patties, chops, salt beef, sausages etc.

VARIATIONS
Cabbage with Cream and Cheese
Cook sliced cabbage until tender in 100ml (4fl oz) water with salt and peppercorns. Mash about 50g (2oz) cream cheese with 100ml (4fl oz) cream. Stir in cabbage, bring to the boil and add seasoning and nutmeg.

Curried Cabbage
Melt 50g (2oz) butter and 1–2 × 5ml tsp (1–2tsp) curry powder over low heat. Toss cabbage in mixture and add 100–200ml (4–7fl oz) chicken stock. Cook until nearly tender under a tight-fitting lid. Then remove lid and allow most of the liquid to evaporate.

Old-fashioned Cabbage Pudding
(serves 4–5)
Preparation time: 20 min
Cooking time: 30–40 min
Oven temperature: 200°C, 400°F, Gas 6
Bottom part of the oven
Suitable for the freezer

1 medium-sized cabbage
50g (2oz) butter
salt, pepper
250g (9oz) pork, minced
2 shallots, 1 egg
2 × 15ml tbsp (2tbsp) flour

Right : Cabbage Roll-ups. Below left : Cabbage Casserole.

100ml (4fl oz) chicken stock
2 × 15ml tbsp (2tbsp) finely chopped pickled gherkins
1 × 5ml tsp (1tsp) cornflour
sherry
brine from gherkins (optional)

1 Shred cabbage finely and brown lightly in butter, a little at a time. Place browned cabbage in a saucepan and add 200–300ml (7–10fl oz) water, 1 × 5ml tsp (1tsp) salt and $\frac{1}{4}$ × 5ml tsp ($\frac{1}{4}$tsp) pepper. Simmer on low heat for about 10 min. Drain cabbage and reserve stock.
2 Mix pork with chopped shallots, egg, flour, stock and gherkins.
3 Place cabbage and mince in layers in a deep, greased ovenproof dish, starting and finishing with cabbage. Add cabbage stock and bake.
4 Pour off meat juices from pudding into a saucepan, bring to the boil and stir in cornflour dissolved in a little cold water. Season with salt, pepper, a dash of sherry and gherkin brine. If the gravy seems pale, add a little gravy browning.

Cabbage Roll-ups
(serves 4–6)
Preparation time: 20 min
Cooking time: about 1 hr
Oven temperature: 200°C, 400°F, Gas 6
Bottom part of the oven
Unsuitable for the freezer

4–6 large potatoes
1 cabbage
salt
250g (9oz) pork, minced
1 onion
1 garlic clove
1 egg
pepper, paprika
2 × 15ml tbsp (2tbsp) flour
100ml (4fl oz) cream
parsley, rosemary
15g ($\frac{1}{2}$oz) butter
about 500ml (1pt) chicken stock
100g ($\frac{1}{4}$lb) bacon

1 Peel potatoes, cut in half lengthways, and make an incision in the cut edges. Steam cabbage for 10 min in lightly salted water, then separate the leaves.
2 Mix together pork, onion, crushed garlic, egg, salt, pepper, paprika, flour, cream, 1 × 15ml tbsp (1tbsp) finely chopped parsley and 1 × 5ml tsp (1tsp) finely chopped fresh, or pinch of dried, rosemary.
3 Sprinkle salt on potatoes and apportion meat mixture over cut edges. Wrap potatoes in cabbage leaves and place in a buttered ovenproof dish.
4 Cut bacon into small pieces and sprinkle over roll-ups. Place dish on the bottom grid of the oven, add stock and cover with tinfoil. Bake until potatoes are soft when pricked with a fork. Meat juices can be thickened with a little cornflour, if liked.

VARIATION
Omit potatoes and allow 500g (1lb 2oz) pork, minced, or 250g (9oz) pork and 250g (9oz) minced beef. The roll-ups can first be fried in butter, then add stock and simmer them gently on top of cooker until tender. If preferred, omit frying process and simmer them in stock without browning them first.

Chinese Cabbage

Chinese cabbage, with its long pale-green, crisp leaves looks rather like cos lettuce. The flavour is delicious, whether eaten raw or cooked.

Chinese Cabbage Salad

(serves 4–6)
Preparation time: 10 min
Unsuitable for the freezer

1 Chinese cabbage
1 cauliflower or 2 stalks of celery
2 mandarin oranges
2 sharp apples
raisins and walnuts (optional)
juice of 1 grapefruit OR 2 lemons
3–4 × 15ml tbsp (3–4tbsp) oil
salt, pepper

1 Cut off base of cabbage, rinse leaves separately, cut into strips and dry in a tea-cloth.
2 Clean cauliflower or celery and cut into small pieces. Divide mandarin oranges into sections and cut apples into cubes.
3 Mix everything in a salad bowl together with raisins and chopped walnuts. Shake together a marinade of grapefruit or lemon juice, oil and seasoning and sprinkle over. Leave salad to settle for about ½ hr.

Chinese Cabbage with Fish Stuffing

(serves 4)
Preparation time: 15 min
Cooking time: about 15 min
Unsuitable for the freezer

2 small Chinese cabbages
salt, pepper
about 200ml (7fl oz) stock
4 small onions
50g (2oz) butter
175g (6oz) mushrooms
1 large can tuna fish
2 eggs, breadcrumbs
1 lemon

1 Rinse Chinese cabbages and cut in half lengthways. Remove base and some inner leaves, but make sure the cabbage does not fall apart. Cut the inner leaves into strips.
2 Place the halved Chinese cabbages in a wide, shallow saucepan with 15g (½oz) butter and stock. Sprinkle with salt and pepper and steam, covered, for 5–6 min.
3 Sauté the chopped onions in 15g (½oz) butter in another saucepan. Add cleaned, coarsely chopped mushrooms and sauté for a couple of minutes. Remove saucepan from heat and mix in flaked fish, cabbage strips and beaten eggs. Add enough breadcrumbs to bind the stuffing together. Season with finely grated lemon rind, lemon juice, salt and pepper.
4 Divide stuffing between the halved cabbages. Sprinkle with remaining butter, melted, and heat for a few minutes with lid on until warmed through.

Chinese Cabbage with Meat Stuffing

(serves 6)
Preparation time: 30 min
Cooking time: about 45 min
Oven temperature: 200°C, 400°F, Gas 6
Bottom grid in the oven
Unsuitable for the freezer

3 small Chinese cabbages
1 quantity forcemeat, as for Stuffed Cabbage (page 15)
25–40 g (1–1½oz) butter
400–500ml (¾–1pt) stock
tomato purée
flour and butter for sauce
salt, pepper
paprika

1 Rinse cabbages and shake off excess water. Cut in half crosswise and hollow out each half.
2 Fill cabbage sections with stuffing and tie round with cotton.
3 Place in an ovenproof dish and sprinkle with melted and lightly browned butter. Bake as directed for 10–15 min. Pour stock into dish, return to oven, and baste frequently until forcemeat is cooked through.
4 Pour off meat juices and bring to the boil with tomato purée, paprika and seasoning. Thicken with equal parts of butter and flour, stirred together and beaten in.

Chinese Cabbage and Spaghetti

(serves 4)
Preparation time: 10 min
Cooking time: about 20 min
Suitable for the freezer

1 large Chinese cabbage
butter
200ml (7fl oz) stock
200g (7oz) spaghetti
150g (5oz) cooked ham
grated cheese
salt, pepper

1 Rinse cabbage, shake off water and cut across into slices. Sauté these in a saucepan for a couple of min in 25–40g (1–1½oz) butter, pour over stock and boil for about 5 min on low heat.
2 Boil spaghetti following instructions on packet. Drain and toss with 1 × 15ml tbsp (1tbsp) melted butter and grated cheese.
3 Mix chopped ham into cabbage and heat everything through. Season to taste. Add spaghetti and mix well. Serve hot.

Chinese Cabbage with Pork

(serves 4)
Preparation time: 15 min
Cooking time: 40–50 min
Suitable for the freezer, but will lose some flavour

50g (2oz) bacon, chopped
2 onions, chopped
400g (14oz) boneless pork
salt, pepper
1 garlic clove
2 carrots, sliced
4 potatoes, cubed
350ml (12fl oz) stock or water
1–2 × 5ml tsp (1–2tsp) caraway seeds or 1 bay leaf
1–2 Chinese cabbages
soy sauce

1 Heat bacon gently in a saucepan to allow fat to run. Add onions and pork, cut into strips, and sauté lightly. Sprinkle with salt and pepper and add crushed garlic, carrots and potato.
2 Pour over stock and add caraway or finely crumbled bay leaf. Simmer, covered, until meat is tender.
3 Rinse cabbage, shake off excess water, and cut across into slices. Add to saucepan and boil for about 8 min. Season with soy sauce.

Clockwise from the top: Chinese Cabbage with Pork; Chinese Cabbage with Meat Stuffing; Chinese Cabbage Salad; Chinese Cabbage and Spaghetti; Chinese Cabbage with Fish Stuffing.

Brussels Sprouts

Brussels sprouts are in season from early autumn until spring. These recipes provide unusual ideas for cooking this familiar vegetable.

Brussels Sprouts in Herb Sauce
(left)
(serves 4)
Preparation time: 20 min
Cooking time: about 20 min
Unsuitable for the freezer

450g (1lb) Brussels sprouts
15g (½oz) butter
150g (5oz) bacon, chopped
2 onions
225g (½lb) button mushrooms
1 lemon
250ml (9fl oz) stock
salt, pepper
cornflour
2 × 15ml tbsp (2tbsp) finely chopped
    herbs

1 Remove any withered leaves from sprouts, then wash. Cook for 8–10 min in lightly salted water. Drain, sauté lightly in butter and keep warm.

2 Fry bacon until crisp and place in saucepan with Brussels sprouts.

3 Sauté chopped onions and whole, cleaned mushrooms in 1–2 × 15ml tbsp (1–2tbsp) melted butter or bacon fat. Lower heat and sprinkle with salt and pepper. Add stock and bring to the boil. Thicken dish with 1–2 × 5ml tsp (1–2tsp) cornflour mixed with a little cold water. Add lemon juice and herbs. Mix sauce with Brussels sprouts and heat through quickly.

Serve with cold meats.

Brussels Sprouts with Meatballs (left)

(serves 4)
Preparation time: 20 min
Cooking time: about 30 min
Suitable for the freezer

450g (1lb) Brussels sprouts
500g (1lb) cooked pork, minced
salt, pepper
about 60g (2½oz) flour
2 eggs
1 small green pepper
3 × 15ml tbsp (3tbsp) finely chopped parsley
about 250ml (9fl oz) milk

25g (1oz) butter
about 150ml (¼pt) single cream

1 Mix pork with 1½ × 5ml tsp (1½tsp) salt, ¼ × 5ml tsp (¼tsp) pepper, 40g (1½oz) flour, lightly beaten eggs, chopped pepper and parsley. Stir in as much milk as needed to bind.

2 Bring lightly salted water to the boil in a saucepan. Shape meat mixture into fairly large balls and boil a few at a time on low heat for about 8–10 min. Remove with a slotted spoon.

3 Clean sprouts, boil for 8–10 min in lightly salted water, then drain.

4 Melt butter, add remaining flour and sauté on low heat for a couple of minutes. Dilute with some of the meat stock until sauce is smooth, then boil for a couple of min and stir in cream and seasoning. Heat sprouts and meatballs in the sauce. Serve with boiled potatoes.

Brussels Sprouts au Gratin

(above)
(serves 4)
Preparation time: 15 min
Cooking time: about 25 min

Suitable for the freezer, but will lose some flavour

450g (1lb) Brussels sprouts
salt, pepper
2–3 onions
25g (1oz) butter
150ml (¼pt) stock
paprika
grated nutmeg
150g (5oz) cooked meat
200ml (7fl oz) sour cream
2 eggs, separated
100g (¼lb) grated cheese

1 Boil the cleaned sprouts for 8–10 min in lightly salted water, then drain.

2 Sauté chopped onion in butter on low heat until shiny. Add stock and boil for 5 min. Add meat, cut into cubes, and nutmeg. Place sprouts in an ovenproof dish and spoon meat mixture over.

3 Mix sour cream with egg yolks and most of the grated cheese. Season with salt, pepper and paprika. Beat egg whites until stiff and fold in. Spread over sprouts, sprinkle with remaining cheese and brown under the grill.

Curly Kale

This dark-green, cabbage-type vegetable is full of vitamin C and iron. It can be a great standby during the darkest winter months and can be frozen satisfactorily. Fresh kale can be kept in plastic in the fridge for 1–2 weeks.

Kale Soup

(serves 6)
Preparation time: 25 min
Cooking time: about 1½ hr
Soup, meat and vegetables without potatoes can be frozen individually

1kg (2¼lb) kale
1kg (2¼lb) salt pork on the bone
salt, black pepper
4–6 carrots
6 potatoes
2–3 leeks
celery tops
sprig of thyme
bunch of parsley
flour to thicken

1 Wash kale well and boil in lightly salted water for 10 min. Drain through a colander and chop coarsely.
2 Place meat in about 2 litres (3½pt) cold water, bring to the boil and skim. Add ½ × 15ml tbsp (½tbsp) salt and ½ × 5ml tsp (½tsp) pepper and simmer, covered, on low heat until meat is tender. For the last 15 min add prepared, sliced vegetables (but

Back : Creamed Kale.
Centre left : Kale with Minced Meat.
Centre right : Casseroled Kale garnished with Poached Eggs.
Front : Thick and filling Kale Soup.

not kale) and a bouquet garni made of leek greenery, celery tops, thyme and parsley.
3 Remove pork, vegetables and bouquet garni. Bring stock to the boil and thicken with 2–3 × 15ml tbsp (2–3tbsp) plain flour stirred into a little cold water. Add chopped kale and season to taste. For a thicker soup, replace some of the meat and vegetables.
Serve soup hot with sliced meat, brown bread and mustard. It can also be served with half a hardboiled egg or one Poached Egg (see this page) per person.
If you happen to have some water that bacon was boiled in, or juices from roasting meats, these can replace some of the water. The soup will then have a much richer flavour.

Creamed Kale

(serves 4–5)
Preparation time: 15 min
Cooking time: about 20 min
Suitable for the freezer

about 700g (1½lb) kale
salt, pepper, nutmeg
40g (1½oz) butter
40g (1½oz) flour
200ml (7fl oz) meat stock
200ml (7fl oz) cream

1 Wash kale well and boil in lightly salted water for 10 min. Drain thoroughly and chop.
2 Melt butter on low heat and stir in flour. Add stock and boil for 8–10 min, stirring constantly. Add cream.
3 Mix in chopped kale and season with salt, pepper and nutmeg.
Serve with boiled salted or cured meat or sausages. Some of the sauce can be flavoured with grated cheese and poured over the sliced meats.

Kale with Minced Meat

(serves 6)
Preparation time: 20 min
Cooking time: about 50 min
Oven temperature: 200–220°C, 400–425°F, Gas 6–7
Bottom grid in the oven
Suitable for the freezer

about 700g (1½lb) kale
2 eggs
1 × 15ml tbsp (1tbsp) breadcrumbs
salt, pepper
nutmeg

3–4 sausages
Meat mixture :
½kg (1lb 2oz) minced meat
salt, pepper, paprika
2–3 eggs
2 × 15ml tbsp (2tbsp) breadcrumbs
1 onion
100ml (4fl oz) single cream

1 Wash kale and boil in lightly salted water for 8–10 min. Drain and chop coarsely. Stir in lightly beaten eggs, breadcrumbs and seasoning to taste.
2 Mix minced meat with seasonings, lightly beaten eggs, grated onion, breadcrumbs and cream.
3 Butter an ovenproof dish well and place in kale, meat mixture, sliced sausages, then kale again. Cover dish with tinfoil and place in preheated oven for 35–40 min until meat is well cooked.
Serve hot with tomato sauce and boiled or fried potatoes.

Casseroled Kale

(serves 4)
Preparation time: 15 min
Cooking time: about 15 min
Suitable for the freezer, but will lose some flavour

about 500g (1lb 2oz) kale
2 onions
40g (1½oz) butter
150ml (¼pt) stock
salt, pepper, paprika
about 400g (14oz) boiled pork

1 Wash kale and boil for 8–10 min. Drain well and chop coarsely.
2 Sauté chopped onion in butter on low heat, add stock and boil for 4–5 min. Add kale, cubed meat and seasonings to taste. Heat through until piping hot. Serve with boiled rice or brown bread and mustard. Garnish with:

Poached Eggs

Bring 1 litre (1¾pt) water with 1 × 5ml tsp (1tsp) salt and 1 × 5ml tsp (1tsp) vinegar to the boil. Crack a fresh egg into a cup and pour it carefully into saucepan when water is boiling. Repeat with other eggs. Gather egg whites around the yolks by means of two spoons. Poach for 3–4 min depending on size.
Remove eggs with slotted spoon, shape edges and keep warm until you are ready to serve them.

Sprouting Broccoli

Sprouting broccoli (calebrese) looks something like cauliflower although its stalk, leaves and 'flower' all have a green or bluish-green colour. The flavour is mild and like asparagus. There is little wastage, for the stalks can be cut small and used with the tops and it does not shrink in cooking.

Boiled Broccoli
(serves 4)
Preparation time: 5 min
Cooking time: 4–8 min
Suitable for the freezer

500g (about 1lb) sprouting broccoli
salt
butter

1 Rinse broccoli well. Slice the stem if it seems hard and tough, and if necessary discard some of the bottom part.
2 Bring water and $\frac{1}{2}$–1 × 5ml tsp ($\frac{1}{2}$–1tsp) salt to the boil in a saucepan. Put in broccoli with the tight, frizzy head showing just above water level. The stalk takes longer to cook than the top which the steam will make tender.
3 Cover and simmer until tender, then drain.
4 Toss well-drained, warm broccoli in 1–2 × 15ml tbsp (1–2tbsp) melted butter. Serve with chopped hard-boiled eggs, or as accompaniment to meat or poultry. Frozen broccoli which has not been defrosted in advance should be cooked in the same way.

Broccoli in Nut Butter (left)
(serves 4)
Preparation time: 15 min
Cooking time: 4–8 min
Unsuitable for the freezer

500g (about 1lb) sprouting broccoli
salt
$\frac{1}{2}$ lemon
75g (3oz) butter
50g (2oz) hazelnuts

1 Wash broccoli and boil in lightly salted water with the juice of $\frac{1}{2}$ lemon.
2 Flake nuts.
3 Brown butter and nuts slightly in a frying pan. Place broccoli on a hot serving dish and pour nut butter over.

Broccoli in Cheese Sauce
(serves 4)
Preparation time: 10 min
Cooking time: about 20 min
Suitable for the freezer

500g (about 1lb) sprouting broccoli
salt, pepper, dry mustard
50g (2oz) butter
2 × 15ml tbsp (2tbsp) flour
300ml ($\frac{1}{2}$pt) stock
100ml (4fl oz) cream
50g (2oz) cream cheese
100g ($\frac{1}{4}$lb) grated cheese

1 Boil washed broccoli until barely tender in lightly salted water. Drain and keep warm.
2 Sauté butter and flour over low heat, then gradually add warm stock and boil for a couple of minutes.
3 Mash cream cheese and beat into sauce with the cream. Remove from heat, add grated cheese and allow it to melt in the sauce. Season with salt, pepper and mustard.
4 Place broccoli on a hot serving dish and pour cheese sauce over. Serve with boiled meat or fish.

French Beans

In summer we can buy fresh, home-produced French beans. For the rest of the year we have to rely on imported, tinned or frozen ones. Fresh beans are suitable for the freezer, but will have to be blanched first.

Beans with Cheese (left)
(serves 4)
Preparation time: 15 min
Cooking time: about 20 min
Oven temperature: 220°C, 425°F, Gas 7
Middle grid in the oven
Suitable for the freezer, but will lose some flavour

500g (about 1lb) French beans
salt, pepper
200g (7oz) cooked meat
200g (7oz) grated cheese
250ml (9fl oz) single cream

1 Wash beans, cook for 5 min in lightly salted water, then drain. Place with sliced meat in a well-greased dish.
2 Mix grated cheese with cream, salt and pepper. Pour into dish and cook in oven until golden brown.

Boiled Green Beans
(serves 4)
Preparation time: 10 min
Cooking time: 10–12 min
Suitable for the freezer, but will lose some flavour

500g (about 1lb) French beans
salt, butter
finely chopped parsley

1 Rinse beans, top and tail. Place in 50–100ml (2–4fl oz) boiling water with $\frac{1}{2} \times 5$ml tsp ($\frac{1}{2}$tsp) salt and $\frac{1}{2}$–1×15ml tbsp ($\frac{1}{2}$–1tbsp) melted butter and cook until tender under a tight-fitting lid.
2 Arrange on a warm serving dish and pour over butter juices. Sprinkle with chopped parsley.

VARIATION (above)
Garnish with plain or butter-steamed tomato wedges and coarsely chopped, hardboiled eggs.

25

Celeriac

This vegetable has delicious flavour and stores well in a cool, dark place or for about two weeks in a fridge. It can be served raw, but is better known boiled and fried in slices or stuffed as in the recipe on this page. Cook celeriac as soon as it is peeled, otherwise its attractive whiteness will discolour.

Stuffed Celeriac

(serves 4)
Preparation time: 25 min
Cooking time: about 1 hr
Oven temperature: 200°C, 400°F, Gas 6
Middle grid in the oven
Unsuitable for the freezer

4 small celeriac
salt, pepper
lemon juice
250g (9oz) minced meat
1 onion, chopped
1 slice of white bread
2–3 × 15ml tbsp (2–3tbsp) tomato
   purée
1 × 5ml tsp (1tsp) mustard
½ × 5ml tsp (½tsp) paprika
1 egg
3–4 ripe tomatoes
300–400ml (½–¾pt) meat stock
parsley, basil, marjoram
1–2 × 5ml tsp (1–2tsp) cornflour

1 Peel celeriac, and immediately place in boiling, lightly salted water with 1 × 15ml tbsp (1tbsp) lemon juice. Cook, covered, on low heat for 15–20 min. Cut off tops and carefully take out insides, leaving a shell ½–1cm (¼–½in) thick.
2 Soak bread in celeriac stock and mix with minced meat, onion, ½ × 5ml tsp (½tsp) salt, ¼ × 5ml tsp (¼tsp) pepper, egg, 1–2 × 15ml tbsp (1–2tbsp) tomato purée, mustard, paprika, 1 × 15ml tbsp (1tbsp) finely chopped parsley or a pinch of dried marjoram and basil. Carefully stir in celeriac stock until stuffing is smooth, but firm.
3 Spoon stuffing into celeriac and place in a greased, ovenproof dish or casserole. Add quartered tomatoes, meat stock and 1 × 15ml tbsp (1tbsp) fresh or 1 × 5ml tsp (1tsp) dried basil. Bake for 30–40 min, basting several times.
4 Strain meat juices, bring to the boil, add remaining tomato purée and season. Thicken with cornflour dissolved in cold water.
Serve hot with sauce or gravy, potato purée, French bread or fried potatoes.

Stuffed Celeriac served with fluffy potato purée and tomato sauce.

Stuffed Celeriac
1 Boil peeled celeriac until tender.

2 Hollow them out with a spoon. Use insides and tops in a soup or sauce.

Celery

A very popular vegetable, whitish-green in colour, with thick, crisp stalks and green leaves. Use in soups and casseroles, or raw in salads. Chilled and crisped in ice-cold water it is a 'must' with cheese. Cut it into chunks, serve with well-flavoured creamed cheese and instantly you have a tasty, healthy snack.

Celery with Herbs
(serves 4)
Preparation time: 20 min
Suitable for the freezer, but will lose some flavour

1 large head of celery
50g (2oz) butter
salt, pepper
200ml (7fl oz) stock
parsley, chives
100–150ml (4–5fl oz) white wine

1 Break stalks apart, rinse well. Cut off rough bottoms of stalks if necessary. Cut into 6–8cm (2–3in) long pieces and put into a saucepan.
2 Sauté in butter until lightly golden, sprinkle with salt and pepper and add stock. Sprinkle with 2–3 × 15ml tbsp (2–3tbsp) finely chopped parsley and chives and simmer, covered, over low heat.
3 Add white wine. Leave uncovered on heat until nearly all the liquid has evaporated.

Celery with Herbs – an interesting way to serve this vegetable.

3 Soak bread in celeriac stock and mix in ingredients for stuffing.

4 Mix stuffing with a little celeriac stock and divide between the celeriac.

5 Bake in a casserole or ovenproof dish and baste with meat juices.

Onions

Raw, boiled, fried, grilled; used whole, sliced or chopped with meat, fish, poultry; or in stuffings, salads, marinades etc – there are no limits to how you can serve onions.

There are many varieties including large, mild, somewhat sweet Spanish onions, stronger and smaller ordinary onions, shallots, spring onions and garlic. We can buy onions all the year round; they keep well and are easy to store.

Whole Fried Onions

(serves 4–5)
Preparation time: 5–10 min
Cooking time: about 15 min
Unsuitable for the freezer

400g (14oz) shallots OR small onions
salt, 25g (1oz) butter

1 Boil onions without peeling them for 5–10 min. Rinse in cold water and peel.
2 Heat butter in a saucepan and toss onions in it until they are nicely golden on all sides. Sprinkle with salt. Serve with roast or other meat dishes.
NOTE Whole, peeled small onions can be placed with roast meats for the last 15–20 min of cooking time.

Glazed Onions

(serves 4–5)
Preparation time: 10 min
Cooking time: about 15 min
Unsuitable for the freezer

400g (14oz) small onions
salt
25g (1oz) butter
1 × 15ml tbsp (1tbsp) sugar

1 Boil onions without peeling them for 10 min or until they are soft. Rinse in cold water and peel.
2 Melt sugar in a heavy pan, add butter and, when butter has stopped sizzling, add onions. Shake pan all the time until onions are shiny and brown. Sprinkle with salt.
Serve with ham, bacon or other cured meats.

Onions with Cheese and Herbs

(serves 4–5)
Preparation time: 10 min
Cooking time: 15–20 min
Suitable for the freezer

500g (1lb 2oz) shallots or small onions
25g (1oz) butter
salt, pepper
100ml (4fl oz) stock
1 × 15ml tbsp (1tbsp) flour
250ml (9fl oz) cream
grated cheese, herbs

1 Scald and peel onions. Sauté in melted butter in a thick-bottomed saucepan on low heat for about 10 min.
2 Sprinkle with salt and pepper, add stock and simmer for about 5 min or until onions are nearly tender.
3 Stir cream into flour and add to the meat juices. Boil for a couple of minutes to thicken, then season.
Serve hot with grated cheese and

sprinkled with finely chopped herbs to taste. Very good with fried meats.

Boiled Onions

Boil large onions, peeled, until soft in butter and a little stock or water with salt added. Or place them in the casserole with beef, veal or poultry.

Stuffed Onions (right)

(serves 4)
Preparation time: 20 min
Cooking time: about 40 min
Oven temperature: 180–190°C, 350–375°F, Gas 4–5
Middle grid of the oven
Unsuitable for the freezer

6–8 large onions
300–400 ml ($\frac{1}{2}$–$\frac{3}{4}$pt) stock
50g (2oz) bacon
250g (9oz) minced meat
salt, pepper, paprika
1 egg
1 garlic clove
4–5 stuffed olives (optional)
grated cheese
40g (1$\frac{1}{2}$oz) butter
1 × 15ml tbsp (1tbsp) flour
100–200ml (4–7fl oz) cream
50g (2oz) cream cheese
chives

1 Boil peeled onions in stock for 10–15 min. Cool and retain stock.
2 Mix together minced meat, finely chopped bacon, seasonings, egg, crushed garlic and chopped olives.
3 Cut top off onions with a sharp knife. Hollow out carefully to leave a neat shell. Chop insides and mix with meat.
4 Spoon stuffing into onions and place in a greased ovenproof dish. Pour some onion stock into dish and cover with tinfoil.
5 Bake for 20–30 min removing tinfoil for the last 5–6 min of cooking time. Sprinkle with grated cheese.

6 Pour meat juices into a saucepan, together with butter and the flour mixed with a little more onion stock, and bring to the boil. Beat cream cheese into sauce, add cream and finely chopped chives. Season to taste.
Serve stuffed onions with sauce and boiled potatoes or with white bread and butter and a salad.

Leeks

These taste delicious and have many other uses besides just being chopped up to add flavour to soups.

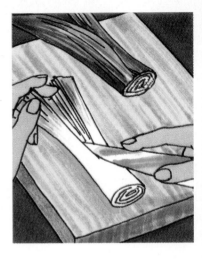

Cleaning Leeks

1 Cut off root and some of the dark green if it seems tough. Remove withered and damaged leaves.

2 Make a long incision each side into the leeks – this is where earth and gravel gather.

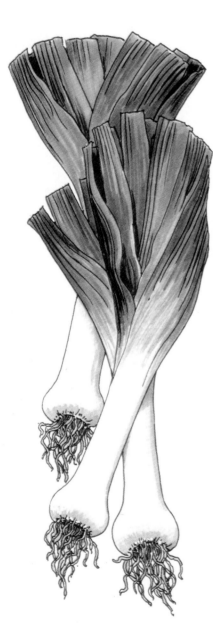

Try butter-steamed leeks with fried or smoked meats, or in green salads, although the mild onion flavour is at its best in egg and cheese dishes. Except for the summer months, leeks are available all the year round, and are excellent for freezing.

In raw salads only the whiter part, sliced into thin rings, is used. The dark-green leaves are used in bouquets garnis or finely chopped in egg dishes. A salad of thin, delicate-tasting leek rings mixed with grapes in a dressing of sour cream is delicious with all kinds of cured meat. Season the sour cream with a dash of nutmeg if liked.

Boiled Leeks

(serves 4)
Preparation time: 10 min
Cooking time: about 10 min
Unsuitable for the freezer

4–8 thick leeks
salt
1 lemon
about 100g ($\frac{1}{4}$lb) butter
white pepper

1 Clean leeks well and boil until barely tender in lightly salted water.

2 Pour off stock, which can be used in soups or sauces later, and steam leeks for a few moments on strong heat.

3 Place the boiled leeks on a hot serving dish preferably on, and covered by, a cloth napkin.

Serve very hot with the butter softened with a little lemon juice and seasoned with white pepper.

In the old days, leeks were boiled this way but for longer, until soft enough to be licked or sucked. They were then eaten with the fingers, as asparagus is today.

Leeks Sautéed in Butter

(serves 4)
Preparation time: 10 min
Cooking time: 4–8 min
Suitable for the freezer, but will lose some flavour

4–8 medium-sized leeks
25g (1oz) butter
salt
100–200ml (4–7fl oz) stock
parsley

1 Cut cleaned leeks into pieces, 6–8cm (2–3in) long.

2 Sauté for a few minutes in butter on low heat, sprinkle with salt and add stock. Boil until leeks are tender, but not too soft.

Serve with finely chopped parsley as accompaniment to fried meats, mince dishes and smoked meats.

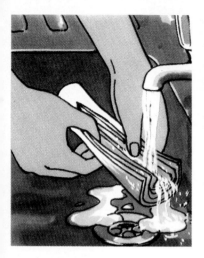

3 Rinse leeks with tops facing down, otherwise sand etc will work further into the leaves.

Leek Pie (right)
(serves 4–5)
Preparation time: 20 min
Cooking time: about 35 min
Oven temperatu.e: 200–220°C,
400–425°F, Gas 6–7
Middle grid in the oven
Uncooked pie is suitable for the freezer

*212g (7½oz) packet frozen puff
    pastry*
8–10 small, thin leeks
25g (1oz) butter
2 × 15ml tbsp (2tbsp) stock
salt, pepper, nutmeg
3 eggs
1 egg yolk
3 × 15ml tbsp (3tbsp) sour cream
*2–3 × 15ml tbsp (2–3tbsp) grated
    cheese*

1 Defrost pastry as instructed on packet.
2 Cut cleaned leeks in half and steam, covered, in butter and stock with seasoning and nutmeg added to taste. Remove cover for the last few minutes to allow liquid to evaporate.
3 Roll out pastry and use most of it to line base and sides of a flan tin. Arrange leeks over base.
4 Beat 2 whole eggs and 1 egg yolk with sour cream, grated cheese and seasoning. Pour egg mixture into tin and cover with a lattice of pastry strips. Brush with beaten egg and bake as directed.

VARIATION
Shortcrust pastry can be substituted for puff pastry. Rub 75g (3oz) butter into 200g (7oz) flour with your fingertips, and add ½–1 × 5ml tsp (½–1tsp) salt. Mix into a dough with 1 lightly beaten egg and 1–2 × 15ml tbsp (1–2tbsp) cold water. Leave to rest in a cold place for ½–1 hr, then roll out and line tin. Prick base well with a fork and bake for 10–12 min at 200°C, 400°F, Gas 6. Place leeks and egg mixture in tin and bake for further 12–15 min.

Leek Rolls

(serves 4)
Preparation time: 15–20 min
Cooking time: about 25 min

6–8 medium-sized leeks
salt, pepper, butter
3 eggs
3–4 × 15ml tbsp (3–4tbsp) flour
250ml (9fl oz) milk
100g (¼lb) cream cheese
3–4 × 15ml tbsp (3–4tbsp) cream

1 Clean leeks and remove the dark-green part. Freeze this, or store in the fridge and use in other recipes.
2 Beat eggs with flour, seasoning and milk and use to make 6–8 small,
thick pancakes.
3 Cook leeks, covered, until barely tender in 1 × 15ml tbsp (1tbsp) butter with salt and water added. Uncover and allow all liquid to evaporate.
4 Roll a pancake round each leek and place carefully in an ovenproof dish. Beat cream cheese with cream until smooth, pour over leeks and place dish under grill until cheese is golden. Serve hot with bread and a salad.

VARIATION
Mix a little tomato purée with a little stock and pour into dish before placing in leek rolls.

Leek Casserole with Pork

(serves 4)
Preparation time: 15 min
Cooking time: about 35 min
Unsuitable for the freezer

300–400g (11–14oz) fresh pork or
bacon
4–5 potatoes
100–200ml (4–7fl oz) stock
salt, pepper
4 medium-sized leeks
200ml (7fl oz) sour cream
paprika, parsley
slices of cheese

1 Cut pork or bacon into cubes, fry lightly and remove from pan. Peel

32

*Three delicious leek dishes. Left:
Leek Rolls. Right: Leeks in Cheese
Sauce. Below right: Leek Casserole
with Pork.*

potatoes and cut into sticks. Clean
leeks and cut into pieces, 3–4cm
(1–1½in) 1ong.

2 Brown potatoes lightly in the
cooking fat from the pork. Pour off
excess fat. Sprinkle with salt and
pepper, add stock and boil for
15–20 min, covered, on low heat.
Add leeks and simmer for 8–10 min.

3 Place meat cubes, potatoes and
leeks in a casserole. Mix sour cream
with salt and pepper to taste and add
plenty of finely chopped parsley.
Pour mixture over and arrange slices
of cheese on top. Place casserole
under grill or in oven with strong
upper heat, until cheese starts to
melt. Sprinkle with paprika. Serve
hot with brown bread.

Leeks in Cheese Sauce

(serves 4–5)
Preparation time: 20 min
Cooking time: about 35 min
Oven temperature: 240°C, 475°F,
Gas 9
Suitable for the freezer, but will lose
some flavour

*8–10 medium-sized leeks
salt, pepper, nutmeg
4–5 slices boiled ham
25g (1oz) butter
2 × 15ml tbsp (2tbsp) flour
100–200ml (4–7fl oz) single cream
1 egg yolk
100–150g (4–5oz) grated cheese*

1 Boil whole cleaned leeks until
barely tender in lightly salted water.
Drain well but keep stock.

2 Melt butter in a thick-bottomed
saucepan on low heat. Stir in flour
and simmer for a couple of min
without browning. Mix in warm
leek stock, a little at a time, until you
have a smooth sauce. Boil for a
couple of minutes and add cream.

3 Remove from heat and beat in egg
yolk and about half the cheese.
Season with salt, pepper and
nutmeg.

4 Roll halved ham slices around
leeks, place them in an ovenproof
dish and pour sauce over. Sprinkle
with the remaining cheese and heat
in oven until cheese melts and goes
lightly golden. Serve with toast or
French bread.

about 700g (1½lb) fresh spinach
50g (2oz) butter
100–150g (4–5oz) flour
100ml (4fl oz) cream
3 eggs
salt, pepper, nutmeg
150g (5oz) Cheddar cheese
50g (2oz) Parmesan cheese

1 Rinse spinach well, remove the coarsest stems and cook for a couple of minutes in the butter. Remove from heat and chop coarsely.
2 Stir in flour, cream, lightly beaten eggs and grated Cheddar cheese. Season with salt, pepper and nutmeg. The mixture should be firm enough to be made into balls. Add more flour if it is too loose.
3 Place a single layer of spinach balls in lightly salted, boiling water for 6–8 min on low heat. Place on a serving dish the moment they are done and keep warm. Sprinkle with grated Parmesan cheese and serve with melted butter as accompaniment to fish or meat.

Spinach Omelette
(serves 4)
Preparation time: 20 min
Cooking time: 6–8 min
Unsuitable for the freezer

1 quantity Creamed Spinach (see
    page 35)
4–6 eggs, separated
2 × 15ml tbsp (2tbsp) flour
salt, pepper, nutmeg
butter, parsley
4 tomatoes

Spinach

Although fresh spinach is available for most months of the year, it can be difficult to find just when you want it. In this case, frozen spinach is an excellent alternative. Allow about three-quarters of frozen to fresh.

Spinach and Cheese Balls
(serves 4)
Preparation time: 20 min
Cooking time: about 20 min
Suitable for the freezer

Spinach and eggs belong together as in Spinach with Ham and Eggs (right). Left: Spinach and Cheese Balls. Below left: Delicious and nourishing Spinach Omelette.

1 Mix cooled creamed spinach with egg yolks, flour and seasoning to taste. Beat egg whites until peaks form and fold carefully into spinach mixture.

2 Fry 4 omelettes in butter. They can be fried on one or both sides.

3 Make incisions in tomatoes and place for a few minutes under grill, or steam, covered, in a little butter in a saucepan. Sprinkle with salt and pepper and garnish with a little parsley.

Serve spinach omelettes freshly made with bread and butter, or with a slice or two of meat.

Butter-steamed Spinach

(serves 4)
Preparation time: 15 min
Cooking time: 6–8 min
Suitable for the freezer, but will lose some flavour

¾–1kg (about 2lb) fresh spinach or
  2 × 350g (12oz) pkt of frozen
15–25g (½–1oz) butter
salt, pepper, nutmeg

Fresh Spinach

1 Remove the coarsest stalks and rinse leaves thoroughly in cold water. Shake off water.

2 Place leaves in a saucepan with butter and steam, covered, on even heat for 6–8 min. Season with salt, pepper and nutmeg.

Frozen Spinach

1 Defrost the frozen spinach and squeeze out all the water.

2 Place in a saucepan with butter. Warm all the way through and season. Serve with meat or fish dishes.

Creamed Spinach

Make 1 quantity of Butter-steamed Spinach following preceding recipe. Coarsely chop the fresh spinach and add 150–200 ml (4–7oz) double cream. Allow to boil for 1–2 min over strong heat, stirring constantly, then season.

Creamed spinach can be made with sour cream or cream cheese.

Spinach with Ham and Eggs

(serves 4)
Preparation time: 15 min
Cooking time: about 30 min
Oven temperature: 220°C, 425°F, Gas 7

1 quantity Butter-steamed Spinach
4–6 thick slices cooked ham
4–6 eggs
25g (1oz) butter
1 × 15ml tbsp (1 tbsp) flour
250ml (9fl oz) stock
100–200ml (4–7fl oz) single cream
salt
pepper
100–150g (4–5oz) grated cheese

1 Place spinach in an ovenproof dish with the slices of ham overlapping in the middle.

2 Boil eggs for 6–8 min and cut in half lengthways. Arrange round edge of dish on top of spinach.

3 Melt butter on low heat and stir in flour. Simmer for a couple of minutes, then add stock and cream to make a smooth sauce. Boil for a couple of min. Remove from heat and stir in half the grated cheese. Season when cheese has melted.

4 Pour sauce over dish, sprinkle with remaining cheese and place high up in the oven until cheese is golden.

Serve piping hot with bread, mustard and a little more grated cheese, if liked.

35

Peas

Fresh garden peas taste delicious but the season is short. However, they freeze exceptionally well and are then available year round. Tinned peas lose much of their flavour and colour.

Peas mix well with everything. Left: Chicken Livers with Peas. Right: Butter-steamed Peas with cubes of cooked smoked ham. Back: Chicken Casserole with Peas.

Butter-steamed Peas

(serves 4)
Preparation time: 15 min
Cooking time: about 15 min
Suitable for the freezer, but will lose some flavour

300–400g (11–14oz) shelled or frozen peas
8–12 shallots
100ml (4fl oz) stock
25g (1oz) butter
salt, chopped parsley

1 Steam, whole, peeled shallots in half the butter and the lightly salted stock for 8–10 min.

2 Add peas and remaining butter and cook, uncovered, for 4–5 min. Season with salt if necessary. Serve sprinkled with finely chopped parsley.

Chicken Livers with Peas

(serves 4)
Preparation time: 15 min
Cooking time: about 20 min
Unsuitable for the freezer

2 onions
25–40g (1–1½oz) butter
curry powder
225g (½lb) chicken livers
225g (½lb) mushrooms

salt, pepper, lemon juice
about 250ml (9fl oz) stock
75g (3oz) long-grain rice
150–200g (5–7oz) shelled OR frozen peas
100ml (4fl oz) double cream or sour cream

1 Dry chicken livers well. Boil rice, cook peas.
2 Sauté onion rings until golden in the butter with a dash of curry powder and place in serving casserole. Sauté livers for a couple of min on both sides on strong heat. Sprinkle with salt and pepper and place in casserole.
3 Sauté cleaned, sliced mushrooms in the fat remaining in pan and season with salt, pepper and lemon juice. Deglaze frying pan with stock and pour into casserole with rice, peas and cream. Heat through on top of stove and season.
Serve with bread and a salad.

Chicken Casserole with Peas

(serves 6)
Preparation time: 20 min
Cooking time: 50–60 min
Unsuitable for the freezer

1 large chicken
salt, pepper, peppercorns
2–3 onions
bouquet garni of leek tops, celery leaves, parsley and thyme
40g (1½oz) rice
15g (½oz) butter
1 garlic clove
150–200g (5–7oz) shelled or frozen peas
100g (¼lb) corn kernels

1 Place chicken in cold water to barely cover. Bring to the boil and skim. Add 1 sliced onion, 2 × 5ml tsp (2tsp) salt, 8 whole peppercorns and bouquet garni. Boil, covered, on low heat until tender. Remove bouquet garni after about 20 min.
2 Take out chicken, remove skin and bones and cut meat into small

36

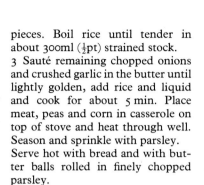

pieces. Boil rice until tender in about 300ml (½pt) strained stock.

3 Sauté remaining chopped onions and crushed garlic in the butter until lightly golden, add rice and liquid and cook for about 5 min. Place meat, peas and corn in casserole on top of stove and heat through well. Season and sprinkle with parsley. Serve hot with bread and with butter balls rolled in finely chopped parsley.

Vegetables in Aspic

(serves 4–6)
Preparation time: 15 min
Cooking time: 6–8 min
Setting time: 2–3 hr
Unsuitable for the freezer

½kg (1lb 2oz) small carrots
1 small cauliflower
350g (¾lb) shelled or frozen peas
1 stock cube
25–40g (1–1½oz) gelatine
Herb Sauce:
100ml (4fl oz) sour cream
200ml (7fl oz) mayonnaise
1 garlic clove
mustard, lemon juice
salt, pepper

about 4 × 15ml tbsp (4tbsp) finely chopped fresh herbs

1 Cut cleaned carrots and cauliflower into small pieces, mix with peas and cook until barely tender in ½ litre (1pt) boiling water to which stock cube and a little lemon juice have been added.
2 Dissolve gelatine in hot water.
3 Drain vegetables through a sieve, retaining liquid, and add dissolved gelatine to this warm vegetable stock. Rinse a ring mould with cold water and pour in about 1cm (½in) of aspic jelly. Put in a cold place to set.
4 Chill remaining jelly until just beginning to thicken and stir in vegetables. Spoon into mould and set firm. Place the cooled mould in warm water for 2–3 sec. Put a plate on top, bottom up, get a firm grip and turn both quickly so that mould is the right way up. Carefully lift it off.
5 Mix sour cream and mayonnaise with crushed garlic, mustard, lemon juice and salt and pepper to taste. Add finely chopped herbs. Spoon sauce into middle of ring or serve separately.

To Shell Peas

1 Use a small knife, get hold of the stem and pull it off.

2 Open the pod with your thumb and carefully prise out peas.

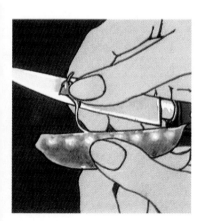

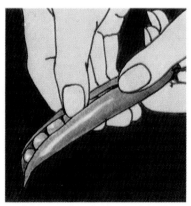

Carrots

This is such a frequently used vegetable that it is not always given the appreciation it deserves. But, available all the year, usable either raw or cooked, with an unusual orange colour which delights the eye, it is difficult to know what we would do without it.

Carrot Salad

(serves 4)
Preparation time: 10 min
Unsuitable for the freezer

4–5 medium carrots
1 lemon
salt, white pepper
200ml (7fl oz) sour cream or natural
*   yoghurt*
fresh dill, parsley, chervil, estragon

1 Scrape or peel carrots, rinse and wrap loosely in plastic. Keep in the fridge overnight, to make them ice-cold and crisp.
2 Grate carrots using the coarsest side of grater and sprinkle with lemon juice. Stir a little lemon juice into sour cream or yoghurt, add seasoning and finely chopped herbs. Pour dressing over carrots.
Serve as a light lunch or as a salad with dinner courses.

Parsley Carrots

(serves 4)
Preparation time: 10 min
Cooking time: about 15 min
Unsuitable for the freezer

10 small carrots or 4–5 large ones
15g (½oz) butter
bunch of parsley
200ml (7fl oz) good stock
salt, pepper
chervil

1 Scrape small carrots or peel large ones. Cut into sticks.
2 Sauté carrots in butter on low heat for a couple of min and pour boiling hot stock over. Rinse parsley and place stalks in saucepan with carrots. Boil, covered, until carrots are barely soft.
3 Remove parsley stalks and taste the carrots. It is often necessary to add more salt, as boiled carrots tend to have a rather sweet flavour. Sprinkle with finely chopped parsley and chervil and serve hot with meat dishes.

Serve Carrots in Lemon Sauce with fried fish.

Carrot Salad is made of ice-cold, crisp carrots.

Carrots and Peas

(serves 4)
Preparation time: 15 min
Suitable for the freezer, but will lose some flavour

½kg (1lb 2oz) small carrots
150g (5oz) shelled peas
salt, white pepper
15g (½oz) butter
1–1½ × 15ml tbsp (1–1½tbsp) flour
100–200ml (4–7fl oz) single cream
finely chopped parsley

1 Cut peeled carrots into small cubes and cook until barely tender in lightly salted water. Add peas for the last 10 min or so. Drain vegetables through a colander but retain stock.
2 Melt butter and stir in flour. Simmer on low heat, but do not allow to brown. Add boiling vegetable stock and cream to make a smooth sauce, then simmer for at least 5 min.
3 Carefully mix drained peas and carrots into the sauce, heat through, season with salt and pepper, and add finely chopped parsley. If you are going to freeze the dish or store it in the fridge, do not add the parsley.
Serve with meat dishes, or mixed with cooked ham in scallop shells or little pastry cases as a first course.

Carrots in Lemon Sauce

(serves 4)
Preparation time: 15 min
Cooking time about 15 min
Unsuitable for the freezer

½kg (1lb 2oz) small carrots
salt, pepper
juice of 1–2 lemons
25g (1oz) butter
1–1½ × 15ml tbsp (1–1½tbsp) flour
200ml (7fl oz) double cream
2 egg yolks
parsley

1 Cut peeled carrots into 3–4cm (1–1½in) long pieces and cook until tender in lightly salted water. Pour off stock and retain.
2 Melt half the butter in a saucepan and stir in flour. Simmer on low heat for a few minutes. Add carrot stock until sauce is smooth and shiny, and boil well for a couple of min.
3 Mix egg yolks with cream, stir in some of the warm sauce, then add to the rest of the warm sauce. Do not allow to boil.
4 Season with lemon juice, salt and white pepper. Whisk in remaining melted and cooled butter and add carrots.
Sprinkle with finely chopped parsley and serve with fried fish or salted or smoked meats.

VARIATION
Flavour sauce with grated cheese instead of lemon. Put carrots in their sauce into an ovenproof dish, sprinkle with grated cheese and place under grill until cheese melts.

Minestrone Soup

(serves 6)
Preparation time: 20 min
Cooking time: 20–25 min
Unsuitable for the freezer

50g (2oz) bacon, cubed
15g (½oz) butter
2 onions
1 garlic clove
4 potatoes, cubed
2 carrots, cubed
salt, pepper
1½–2 litres (2½–3½pt) meat stock
1–2 courgettes
2 stalks of celery
1–2 thin leeks
4–5 ripe tomatoes
100g (4oz) shelled or frozen peas
50g (2oz) rice, cooked
grated Parmesan cheese

1 Sauté bacon cubes in butter in a large saucepan until golden. Add coarsely chopped onions, crushed garlic, potatoes and carrots. Mix well. Add stock and boil on low heat for about 10 min.
2 Wash courgettes and cut in four lengthways. Cut these pieces into small slices, place in a colander, sprinkle with salt and leave for 10 min.
3 Meanwhile boil sliced celery stalks and leek rings for about 5 min with the other vegetables in the pot. Rinse and dry courgettes and add together with the sliced peeled tomatoes, peas and cooked rice. Boil until everything is barely tender. Season with salt and pepper and sprinkle with 1–2 × 15ml tbsp (1–2tbsp) grated Parmesan cheese. Serve soup with brown bread and a dish of grated cheese.

Minestrone – the Italian vegetable soup – is served with a sprinkling of grated Parmesan cheese.

Vegetable Soups and Hotpots

It is the variety of vegetables in these recipes that makes them so tasty – and just the thing to warm you up on cold winter days.

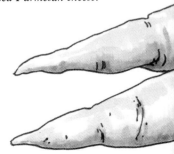

Vegetarian Hotpot with Eggs

(serves 4)
Preparation time: 15 min
Cooking time: about 30 min
Unsuitable for the freezer

3 onions
6 potatoes
2 carrots
40g (1½oz) butter
2 thin leeks or ½ stalk of celery
salt, pepper, paprika
250g (9oz) mushrooms
250g (9oz) shelled or frozen peas
sprig of parsley
4 eggs

1 Fry onion rings, potato in small cubes and sliced carrots in half the butter on strong heat.
2 Season with salt, pepper and paprika. Lower heat and fry, covered, for further 10 min. Add leek rings or sliced celery and simmer until not quite tender. Add peas and simmer until tender. Add stock or water if vegetables look dry.
3 Sauté cleaned sliced mushrooms in remaining butter and sprinkle with salt and pepper. Mix with the other vegetables. Season with paprika and sprinkle with finely chopped parsley. Fry eggs and arrange on top of vegetables.
Serve with brown bread, mustard and pickled gherkins.

Winter Hotpot

(serves 4)
Preparation time: 15–20 min
Cooking time: about 20 min
Unsuitable for the freezer

2 onions
4 potatoes
¼ of a celeriac
2 carrots
1 wedge of hearted cabbage
25g (1oz) butter
salt, pepper
200–300ml (7–10fl oz) stock
3–4 thin leeks
1 red pepper
50g (2oz) cream cheese
½–1 × 15ml tbsp (½–1 tbsp) made mustard
finely chopped parsley

1 Clean all vegetables and cut into small pieces.
2 Sauté onions, potatoes, celeriac, carrots and cabbage in butter in a saucepan for 4–5 min. Season with salt and pepper, add stock and simmer, covered, for about 10 min.
3 Add leeks and red pepper to saucepan and boil for 4–5 min. Mix cream cheese and mustard with a little liquid from saucepan, then stir into vegetables. Season with salt and sprinkle generously with parsley. Serve hotpot on its own or with meat.

These recipes show how different vegetables can be combined to provide a delicious and colourful medley. But don't only use the vegetables suggested – be adventurous and experiment for yourself. And make use of vegetables which are in season and therefore cheap.

Cucumber

Cucumber is in the shops all the year round. It is most frequently used for salads, in sandwiches and as decoration, but it also makes many hot, tasty dishes.

Devilled Cucumber

(serves 4)
Preparation time: 15 min
Cooking time: about 10 min
Unsuitable for the freezer

2 cucumbers
salt, pepper
2–3 × 15ml tbsp (2–3tbsp) oil
1 lemon

Mustard and chives add a nice flavour to Devilled Cucumber.

1–2 × 15ml tbsp (1–2tbsp) made
  mustard
50–100ml (2–4fl oz) dry white wine
  or stock
chives

1 Wash cucumbers and cut into fairly thick slices. Place in a colander, sprinkle with a little salt, and leave for 5–10 min.
2 Mix oil, lemon juice, mustard and wine or stock in a shallow, wide saucepan or frying pan. Dry cucumbers, place in pan and cook until barely tender.
3 Season with pepper and a little more salt and sprinkle with finely chopped chives.
Serve either hot or cold with meat or fish.

Cucumber in Dill Sauce

(serves 4)
Preparation time: 15 min
Cooking time: about 10 min
Unsuitable for the freezer

1 large cucumber
1 × 15ml tbsp (1tbsp) flour
250ml (9fl oz) cream
15g (½oz) butter
salt, dill

1 Peel and slice cucumber. Remove seeds and cut flesh into sticks. Place in a sieve or colander, sprinkled with a touch of salt, for 5–10 min.
2 Cook cucumber until tender in enough unsalted water to barely cover them. Remove with a slotted spoon and place in a warm dish.
3 Stir flour into cream with a little cucumber stock, add to the rest of the cooking liquid and beat in melted, cooled butter. Season sauce with salt and finely chopped dill. Serve this dish with meat or fish.

Greek Cucumber Salad

(serves 4)
Preparation time: 15 min
Unsuitable for the freezer

1 small cucumber
salt, pepper
100–200ml (4–7fl oz) natural
  yoghurt
1 × 15ml tbsp (1tbsp) oil
1 × 15ml tbsp (1tbsp) lemon juice
1 garlic clove
chives

1 Wash cucumber and cut into sticks. It is not necessary to peel it unless the skin is coarse or tough. Place sticks in a sieve or colander, sprinkle with a touch of salt, and leave for 5–10 min.
2 Make a dressing of yoghurt, oil, lemon juice, crushed garlic, salt, pepper and finely chopped chives. Mix in cucumber sticks.
Serve cold as an accompaniment to mutton or poultry.

Cucumber and Kidneys

(serves 4)
Preparation time: 1 hr
Cooking time: about 30 min
Oven temperature: 200–220°C, 400–425°F, Gas 6–7
Middle part of the oven
Unsuitable for the freezer

*300–400g (11–14oz) lamb's kidneys
vinegar
2 large cucumbers
juice of 1 lemon
salt, pepper, paprika
50g (2oz) bacon, cubed
15g (½oz) butter
2 onions
200ml (7fl oz) dry white wine or
    stock
2 × 15ml tbsp (2tbsp) finely chopped
    parsley and dill
about 100g (¼lb) cheese, grated*

1 Clean kidneys and cut in half. Rinse well and soak in a little cold water with 1 × 5ml tsp (1tsp) added vinegar for about 1 hr.

2 Peel cucumbers and cut lengthways. Scrape out seeds and loose flesh. Sprinkle with lemon juice and salt and pepper. Place in a greased ovenproof dish.

3 Sauté bacon cubes lightly and place on kitchen paper to drain. Raise heat and sauté chopped onion and sliced, well-drained kidneys in butter.

4 Mix bacon, onion and kidneys. Season and add 3–4 × 15ml tbsp (3–4tbsp) wine or stock and finely chopped herbs. Spoon into cucumbers, pour the remaining wine or stock into dish and cover with foil.

5 Bake as directed, the last 10–15 min without foil and sprinkled with the grated cheese. Serve with boiled potatoes and Tomato Sauce (see below).

*Cucumber and Kidneys, with mushrooms added, makes a good supper snack.
Left: Cucumber in Dill Sauce.*

VARIATION
You can also stuff the cucumbers as in the recipe for courgettes on page 56.

Tomato Sauce
Melt 20g (¾oz) butter, stir in 2 × 15ml tbsp (2tbsp) flour together with stock or tomato juice and any meat juices from frying, about 400ml (¾pt) in all. Boil for 3–4 min and add tomato purée, salt, pepper and a little sugar to taste.

Easy-to-make Tomato Sauce
Concentrated canned tomato soup can be used as sauce. Heat it and add flavouring to taste.

Chicory

Chicory or Belgian endive is oval-shaped, with tightly packed crisp leaves. Raw, it lends itself to salads, but its distinctive taste is equally valuable in hot dishes.

Braised Chicory
(serves 4)
Preparation time: 5 min
Cooking time: 10–20 min
Unsuitable for the freezer

4 medium-sized heads of chicory
25g (1oz) butter
salt, pepper
200ml (7fl oz) white wine or stock
lemon juice
parsley

1 Tear off withered leaves, if any.

Trim root and as much as possible of the small, inner core. Rinse quickly.
2 Place chicory and butter in a wide, shallow saucepan or frying pan. Cook on moderate heat, turning chicory often until golden all over. Lower heat a little, season with salt and pepper and add white wine or stock with a little lemon juice.
3 Cook, covered, until barely tender. Remove lid for the last few min of cooking time.
Garnish with parsley and serve with poultry, pork, mutton or veal.

Chicory with Ham and Cheese

(serves 4)
Preparation time: 15 min
Cooking time: about 30 min
Oven temperature: 220°C, 425°F,
Gas 7
Middle part of the oven
Suitable for the freezer, but will lose
some flavour

6 heads of chicory
juice of 1 lemon

salt, pepper, paprika
15g (½oz) butter
1–1½ × 15ml tbsp (1–1½tbsp) flour
200ml (7fl oz) single cream
200g (7oz) cheese
225g (½lb) cooked ham, cubed

1 Clean chicory and cook for 5 min
in lightly salted water with lemon
juice added. Place in an ovenproof
dish and retain cooking water.
2 Melt butter, stir in flour and
simmer on low heat without browning. Add cream and cooking water
until sauce is smooth. Remove from
heat and stir in about 100g (¼lb)
grated cheese. Season with salt and
pepper.
3 Place ham cubes in dish with
chicory and pour sauce over. Slice
remaining cheese and arrange on
top. Put dish in oven until cheese
has melted. Sprinkle with paprika
and serve with bread and a salad.

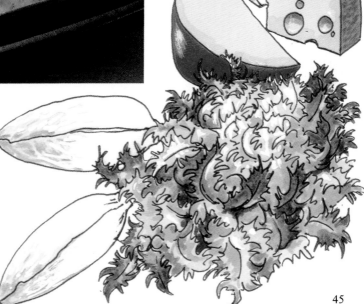

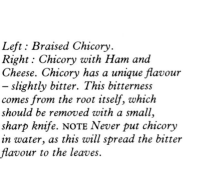

Left: Braised Chicory.
Right: Chicory with Ham and
Cheese. Chicory has a unique flavour
– slightly bitter. This bitterness
comes from the root itself, which
should be removed with a small,
sharp knife. NOTE *Never put chicory*
in water, as this will spread the bitter
flavour to the leaves.

Asparagus

Fresh asparagus is a real delicacy, to be treated carefully. It is usually available in late spring and early summer.

To Clean Asparagus

The bottom of the stalk is often woody and should be cut off. Use this and scrapings for soup or boil to make stock to cook asparagus in. Scrape the white part of the stalk gently with a knife – to avoid damaging the coloured tips, work from the top down. There are many varieties of asparagus and new ones, for instance from Italy, are being introduced to this country. White asparagus is shown on page 47.

Boiled Asparagus

Tie asparagus in bunches with tape or thin strips of tinfoil. Place in a tall, narrow saucepan or at an angle in an ordinary saucepan so that the tops are above water. They need a shorter boiling time than the stalks and the steam makes them tender.

Pour boiling, lightly salted water (or stock from discarded asparagus) over and boil for 12–15 min according to size.

Remove bunches with a slotted spoon. Drain stalks thoroughly in a hot dish with a tea towel wrapped round them. This way all excess fluid will be soaked up and the asparagus kept warm.

Use stock from boiling for soups, sauces, stews etc, or freeze for later use.

Asparagus as a Starter

Serve the asparagus piping hot with lemon wedges and melted butter. Allow 6–10 stalks per person depending on thickness. Accompany with thin slices of hot cooked ham.

Asparagus Soup

(serves 4)
Cooking time: 7–12 min
Unsuitable for the freezer

½kg (1lb 2oz) asparagus, sliced
2–3 egg yolks
250ml (9fl oz) cream
200g (7oz) can small meatballs
salt, pepper, nutmeg
a little dry sherry

1 Boil asparagus in ¾–1 litre (about 1½pt) lightly salted water for about 7 min. Remove with a slotted spoon.
2 Beat egg yolks with a little warm asparagus stock and add to the saucepan. Beat in cream and keep soup just below boiling point. Add asparagus and about 200g (7oz)

small meatballs and allow them to get warm all the way through. Season soup with salt, pepper, nutmeg and a dash of dry sherry.

French Asparagus (left)
Boil ¾–1kg (about 2lb) asparagus. Bake 2 slices of bread, crusts removed. Crush into crumbs and fry until golden in 1 × 15ml tbsp (1tbsp) melted butter. Sprinkle crumbs, 3–4 × 15ml tbsp (3–4tbsp) grated Emmenthaler cheese and 2 × 15ml tbsp (2tbsp) finely chopped parsley over the warm asparagus. Finally pour over 2 × 15ml tbsp (2tbsp) lemon juice and 75–100g (3–4oz) melted butter.

Right : The asparagus season is short, enjoy it while it lasts.
Below : Asparagus Soup can be made from either fresh or canned asparagus. Meatballs make it tasty and filling.

Mushrooms

Nowadays cultivated mushrooms are available all the year round, though the price may vary a little. Fresh, unwashed mushrooms with the stalks cut off will keep for 3–4 days in the fridge, loosely wrapped in plastic.

Cleaning Mushrooms

Cultivated button mushrooms need little cleaning. Just cut off the tips of the stalks and gently rub or wash caps. More open ones, and certainly field mushrooms, have to be peeled. Get a knife under the outside edge of the cap and peel towards the centre. Never leave mushrooms in water as they go soft and deteriorate in flavour. Raw mushrooms can be used in salads. Sprinkle them with lemon juice to avoid discoloration.

Buttered Mushrooms

(serves 4)
Preparation time: 10 min
Cooking time: 6–8 min
Suitable for the freezer, but will lose some flavour

½kg (about 1lb) mushrooms
25g (1oz) butter
salt, pepper
lemon juice, parsley

1 Cut cleaned mushrooms into slices and cook in butter on moderate heat.
2 Season and add a little lemon juice. Sprinkle with finely chopped parsley.

Mushrooms in Cream

(serves 4)
Preparation time: 10 min
Cooking time: 6–8 min
Suitable for the freezer, but will lose some flavour

½kg (about 1lb) mushrooms
25g (1oz) butter
salt, pepper
1 × 15ml tbsp (1tbsp) flour
½ lemon
300–400 ml (½–¾pt) cream
parsley

1 Cook cleaned, sliced or whole small mushrooms in butter for 2–3 min. Add salt, pepper and flour.
2 Stir in lemon juice and cream and boil for 4–5 min on low heat, stirring from time to time. Sprinkle with finely chopped parsley just before serving.

VARIATION
Mushrooms au Gratin
Make 1 quantity of Mushrooms in Cream and mix in small cubes of cooked meat. Sprinkle with grated cheese and place under the grill or in oven set at 240°C, 475°F, Gas 9 until cheese melts and becomes golden.

Mushroom Soup
Make 1 quantity of Mushrooms in Cream and mix in about 1 litre (1¾pt) of chicken stock. Bring to the boil and season to taste.

Top: Buttered Mushrooms flavoured with lemon juice. Above: Mushrooms in Cream.

Left: Different ways of using mushrooms in cooking. The recipe for Mushroom Soup is given above, but here are some more suggestions for you to try for yourself. Clockwise from top left: Rolls of ham stuffed with creamed mushrooms; Mushroom Soup; Mushrooms in Cream with bacon, tomato slices and cheese; raw, sliced mushrooms in a salad; cream-stewed mushrooms with grated cheese.

Potatoes

The potato is one of the most commonly used vegetables — it appears on the dinner table in some form or other nearly every day. But, do we take full advantage of the possible variations? On the following pages we try to give you suggestions and ideas.

The first new potatoes in the spring are something special, but potatoes provide a good basis in our diet all year round. There are many varieties. The firm ones are best for boiling; large, mealy potatoes are best for purées or baking.

Potatoes Anna

(serves 4)
Preparation time: 20 min
Cooking time: 1½–2 hr
Oven temperature: 150–160°C, 300–325°F, Gas 2–3
Bottom part of the oven
Unsuitable for the freezer

1kg (2¼lb) large potatoes
about 100g (¼lb) butter
salt, pepper, breadcrumbs

1 Peel, rinse and dry potatoes and slice thinly.
2 Butter 1 large or 4 small soufflé dishes, sprinkle with breadcrumbs.
3 Place potato slices in layers in dish(es) with salt, pepper and butter in thin slices. Press potato slices well together, place butter on the top and place dish(es) in the oven.
4 Bake as directed, pressing potato slices together several times during baking.
Turn out onto a hot dish. When serving, slice like a cake. Serve with any meat or fish.

Potatoes Fried in Butter

(serves 4)
Preparation time: 10 min
Cooking time: 10–20 min
Unsuitable for the freezer

½–¾kg (1¼–1½lb) potatoes
1 × 15ml tbsp (1tbsp) butter
1 × 15ml tbsp (1tbsp) oil
salt

1 Peel potatoes and dry them. Medium-sized potatoes should be cut into fairly thick fingers, small potatoes left whole.
2 Fry sliced potatoes in butter in a large frying pan on moderate heat.

In oblong dishes clockwise:
Matchsticks, Potatoes Fried in
Butter, Potato Chips and Game
Chips.
Bottom left: Potatoes Anna.
Bottom right: Potato Soufflés.

Turn often and sprinkle with salt.
3 Fry small, whole potatoes in half oil and half butter. Shake pan to make potatoes brown and tender. Sprinkle with salt when done.

Potato Chips

(serves 4)
Preparation time: 20 min
Cooking time: about 4 min per portion
Suitable for the freezer after first frying process

½–¾kg (1¼–1½lb) potatoes
oil or lard
salt

1 Peel, rinse and dry potatoes and cut into sticks.
2 Heat oil or lard in a chip pan to about 180°C, 350°F, (a small cube of crustless white bread goes brown in 1 min).
3 Place a single layer of potatoes at a time in the chip pan. Turning from time to time, fry for 2–3 min, depending on size. When lightly golden, place on kitchen paper to drain.
4 Just before serving heat oil or lard to 200°C, 400°F, and fry potatoes until golden brown. You can now put a larger quantity of chips in at a time. Drain on kitchen paper and sprinkle with salt.

Game Chips and Matchsticks

Game Chips: Slice peeled potatoes into paper-thin slices on a grater or with a sharp knife.
Matchsticks: Slice potatoes into tiny strips.
Rinse and dry as for Potato Chips, fry only once at 200°C, 400°F. Do not put too many at a time into the chip pan.

Potato Soufflé

Mix ½kg (1lb 2oz) boiled, mashed potatoes with 50ml (2fl oz) double cream, 4 egg yolks, 50–75g (2–3oz) grated cheese, finely chopped chives, salt and pepper. Beat 4 egg whites until peaks form and fold in carefully. Pour soufflé into one large or several small, well-greased soufflé dishes, sprinkled with breadcrumbs. Bake the large dish at 200°C, 400°F, Gas 6 for 25–30 min and small ones for 15–20 min at 220°C, 425°F, Gas 7. Serve with butter as accompaniment.

Above : New potatoes served with fresh dill are a delicacy.
Later in the year variety will be welcomed – the possibilities are many. Boil a
double quantity and make Potato Croquettes (below) or Potato Cakes. Left-
overs can be steamed in lightly salted water – they will be as good as 'new'.

Baked Jacket Potatoes
(serves 6)
Preparation time: 5 min
Oven temperature: 200–220°C,
400–425°F, Gas 6–7
Middle part of the oven
Unsuitable for the freezer

6 very large or 12 medium-sized
potatoes
Filling : see suggestions

1 Brush potatoes until completely
clean and dry on kitchen paper.
Prick with a fork to prevent skin
from cracking while cooking.
2 Place potatoes directly on a baking sheet, in an ovenproof dish or in
a roasting tin. Brush with oil, as this
makes skin crisp and tasty. Or you
can wrap the potatoes in tinfoil.
This does not help the baking in any
way, but the skin becomes soft and is
easier to pull apart.
3 Poke a thin knitting needle to the
middle of the potatoes to see if they
are soft. Cooking time depends on
their size, and also on the kind of
potato. Squeeze the cooked potatoes
carefully, or make a cross-like incision and pull the skin apart a little.
Hold potatoes in an oven glove to
prevent burning your fingers. Spoon
filling (see below) into each potato,
or just a dollop of butter.

Suggestions for Filling
200ml (7fl oz) sour cream, seasoned
with lemon juice, salt and pepper.
Place a touch of red or black caviar
on top.

100g ($\frac{1}{4}$lb) butter, softened with
1 × 15ml tbsp (1tbsp) red wine or
tomato purée and a generous
amount of paprika. Roll butter to a
sausage shape, and put in a cold
place. Cut into slices.

100g ($\frac{1}{4}$lb) cottage cheese mixed with
salt, pepper, crushed garlic and
about 3 × 15ml tbsp (3tbsp) finely
chopped fresh herbs.

100g ($\frac{1}{4}$lb) chilled butter, cut into
fingers or cubes and rolled in finely
chopped parsley.

100g ($\frac{1}{4}$lb) fresh cream cheese, stirred until smooth with 1–2 × 15ml
tbsp (1–2tbsp) cream, mustard and
3–4 × 15ml tbsp (3–4tbsp) finely
chopped cress.

Puréed Potatoes

(serves 4)
Preparation time: 15 min
Cooking time: about 20 min
Unsuitable for the freezer

¾–1kg (about 2lb) mealy potatoes
about 300ml (½pt) milk
salt, pepper
25g (1oz) butter

1 Peel potatoes and boil in unsalted water until soft. Pour off water and steam potatoes until dry.
2 Mash potatoes. Beat up purée with boiling milk until you get the right consistency.
3 Season with salt and pepper and stir in butter.
NOTE The purée will be dry and heavy if potatoes are boiled in salted water or beaten with cold milk. Serve with casseroles, sausages etc.

Baked Puréed Potatoes

Beat mashed, boiled potatoes with 2 whole eggs, 1 extra egg yolk, 25g (1oz) butter, salt and pepper. Place in an ovenproof dish and brown under grill or in the oven at 220–240°C, 425–475°F, Gas 7–9.

Potato Croquettes

(serves 4)
Preparation time: 1¼–2¼ hr
Cooking time: 3–5 min per portion
Suitable for the freezer

1 quantity Puréed Potatoes
1 shallot, nutmeg
1 egg, flour, breadcrumbs
oil or lard

1 Season purée with grated or finely chopped shallot and a good pinch of grated nutmeg. Spread out evenly on a flat dish and cool completely.

Baked Jacket Potatoes with a delicious filling of cottage cheese and fine herbs.

2 With floured hands, shape into oblong croquettes. Turn these in flour, then in beaten egg, and finally in breadcrumbs.
3 Heat oil or lard in a chip pan to 180–190°C, 350–375°F and place in 3–5 croquettes at a time. Remove with a slotted spoon and drain on kitchen paper as you go along. Sprinkle with salt.

53

1 Peel potatoes and grate coarsely. Squeeze out moisture. Coarsely grate peeled onion and mix with potatoes. Beat eggs and cream together, add salt and pepper and stir in potatoes and onion.
2 Brown butter in a large frying pan and put in 4 large spoonfuls of potato mixture. Shape into round cakes with a spatula. Fry for 4–6 min on each side.

Cheesy Potatoes

(serves 4)
Preparation time: 10 min
Cooking time: about 25 min
Unsuitable for the freezer

¾–1kg (about 2lb) firm potatoes
salt, pepper
200g (7oz) cheese

1 Boil potatoes in their skins. Rinse in cold water and peel them. Cut in thick slices and season.
2 Place potatoes in a greased, ovenproof dish and place slices of cheese on top. Place under grill or in the oven at a temperature of 240°C, 475°F, Gas 9 until cheese has melted and is lightly golden.

Potato Cakes

1kg (2¼lb) peeled potatoes, boiled in
*   unsalted water*
1 × 5ml tsp (1tsp) salt
about 250g (9oz) flour

1 Purée potatoes and salt.
2 Mix enough flour with the potato mixture to form a dough.
3 Roll out to about 3cm (1in) thick, and cut out cakes about 15cm (6in) in diameter.
4 Fry on a hotplate or griddle, or in a dry frying pan. Wrap in a cloth immediately they are cooked.

Butter-baked Potatoes

(serves 4)
Preparation time: 15 min
Cooking time: 45–60 min
Oven temperature: 200°C, 400°F, Gas 6
Middle part of the oven
Unsuitable for the freezer

8–12 medium-sized, preferably
*   oblong, potatoes*
salt, pepper
50–75g (2–3oz) butter
breadcrumbs
grated cheese (optional)

Potato Salad

(serves 4)
Preparation time: 10 min
Cooking time: 15–20 min
Unsuitable for the freezer

½kg (1lb 2oz) firm potatoes
4 shallots
1 garlic clove
100ml (4fl oz) dry white wine
sprig of fresh or ½ × 5ml tsp (½tsp)
*   dried, thyme*
1 small can anchovy fillets
salt, pepper, chives
1 × 15ml tbsp (1tbsp) wine vinegar
1 × 15ml tbsp (1tbsp) olive oil

1 Boil potatoes in their skins. Rinse with cold water and peel.
2 Meanwhile boil coarsely chopped shallots and crushed garlic in white wine with fresh or dried thyme.

3 Cut the warm potatoes into slices and pour the warm wine mixture over. Cool salad.
4 Place the well-drained anchovy fillets on top of the potatoes. Shake together a marinade of wine vinegar, oil, salt, pepper and finely chopped chives. Sprinkle over salad.
Serve with fried or grilled meats or poultry.

Small Potato Pancakes

(serves 4)
Preparation time: 15 min
Cooking time: 8–12 min
Unsuitable for the freezer

¾–1kg (about 2lb) potatoes
1 large onion
salt, pepper, 4 eggs
100ml (4fl oz) cream
butter for frying

Left: Potato Salad is a meal in itself, but is also a good accompaniment to other dishes.
Below: Small Potato Pancakes, delicious with fried bacon and tomatoes, or with salad. It is economical too.
Right: Cheesy Potatoes – easy to make and very tasty.

1 Peel and dry potatoes. Cut across in slices without cutting all the way through. (Slices should hang together at the bottom.) It is easiest to place potato in a deep spoon and cut down to the edge, or to poke a skewer lengthways through the potato and cut down as far as this. The potatoes can also be placed next to a bread board and cut down to this.

2 Place potatoes in greased ovenproof dish or small roasting tin. Sprinkle with salt and pepper. Place butter in thin slices on top, or brush with melted butter. Bake until golden brown and soft. Spoon butter over during baking. Sprinkle with a few breadcrumbs and grated cheese during the last 10–15 min of cooking time.
Serve piping hot.

Potatoes au Gratin
(serves 4–5)
Preparation time: 15 min
Cooking time: 45–60 min
Oven temperature: 200°C, 400°F, Gas 6
Middle part of the oven
Unsuitable for the freezer

1kg (2¼lb) potatoes
1 garlic clove
2–3 onions
salt, pepper
75–100g (3–4oz) butter
200g (7oz) grated cheese
250ml (9fl oz) double cream
200–300ml (7–10fl oz) milk or single cream

1 Peel, rinse and dry potatoes and cut into strips or thin slices. Cut onions into thin rings.

2 Rub an ovenproof dish with the cut edge of half a garlic clove or crush it and mix in with other ingredients. Grease dish well with butter. Place potato slices overlapping in dish, in layers with onions, butter in thin slices and most of the cheese. Season each layer with salt and pepper.

3 Pour double cream over and sprinkle with the remaining cheese. Place thin slices of butter on top and bake as directed. Add milk or cream after a while, to prevent dish going dry.
Serve immediately with any meat or poultry dish.

VARIATION
Anchovy Potatoes
Replace cheese with anchovy fillets between potato layers.

Left : Courgettes with Cheese. Right
from above : Stuffed Courgettes,
Fried Aubergines and Aubergines in
Meat Sauce.

Courgettes and Aubergines

Courgettes, also called zucchini, resemble cucumber, but the flesh is softer and has a delicate, creamy colour. Use raw in salads, cooked as a hot vegetable, in soups and in casseroles.

Aubergine, or egg plant, is mostly used in casseroles and gratins. Always sprinkle raw aubergine or courgette slices with salt, leave for a while and dry well, before frying. Both vegetables can be cut into slices or sticks and deep-fried or baked in oil.

Boiled Courgettes
(serves 4)
Preparation time: 15 min
Cooking time: 6–8 min
Suitable for the freezer, but will lose some flavour

4–6 courgettes ($\frac{1}{2}$–$\frac{3}{4}$kg; about $1\frac{1}{2}$lb)
salt, pepper, parsley
25g (1oz) butter
100ml (4fl oz) stock

1 Wash courgettes and top and tail. Cut into slices, sprinkle with salt and place in a colander for about 10 min.
2 Rinse and dry well. If you use coarse salt, just dry them.
3 Sauté courgettes lightly in butter

in a saucepan. Add stock and simmer on low heat until they are just soft. Season with pepper.
Serve sprinkled with finely chopped parsley.

VARIATION
Courgettes with Cheese
Place the above quantity of boiled courgettes in an ovenproof dish. Mix 100g ($\frac{1}{4}$lb) cream cheese with boiling courgette stock, 100–200ml (4–7fl oz) single cream, 2 finely chopped shallots and 100–150g (4–5oz) cheese cut into cubes. Spoon over courgettes.
Bake for 10–15 min at 200–220°C, 400–425°F, Gas 6–7.

Stuffed Courgettes
(serves 4)
Preparation time: 20 min
Cooking time: 25–30 min
Oven temperature: 200°C, 400°F, Gas 6
Middle part of the oven
Unsuitable for the freezer

4 large courgettes
salt, pepper, paprika
1 onion
25g (1oz) butter
250g (9oz) minced meat
2 eggs
slice of white bread
parsley
fresh or dried basil
100ml (4fl oz) stock

1 Wash courgettes and cut lengthways. Remove pips, scrape out some of the flesh and finely chop. Sprinkle salt on cut edges and place uncut side up.
2 Sauté chopped onion in 15g ($\frac{1}{2}$oz) butter. Add mince, breaking it up with a fork. Remove from heat and stir in seasonings, crumbled bread, lightly beaten eggs and finely chopped herbs.
Stuff courgettes with mince mixture and place in a greased ovenproof dish. Pour in stock and bake as directed.
Serve hot with bread and a salad.

Fried Aubergines

(serves 4)
Preparation time: 1 hr 5 min
Cooking time: 4–5 min
Unsuitable for the freezer

2 aubergines
salt, olive oil

1 Wash aubergines, remove stalks and cut, lengthways or across, into slices about 1cm ($\frac{1}{2}$in) thick.
2 Sprinkle with coarse salt and leave in a cool place for about 1 hr.
3 Remove salt with kitchen paper and fry slices in olive oil on moderate heat until golden. Drain on kitchen paper. Serve hot with fried meat dishes, accompanied by Tomato Sauce (see page 43 for recipe).

Aubergines in Meat Sauce

(serves 4)
Preparation time: 20 min
Cooking time: about 20 min
Oven temperature: 200–220°C, 400–425°F, Gas 6–7
Middle part of the oven
Unsuitable for the freezer

2 small aubergines
salt, pepper, paprika
3–4ml tbsp (3–4tbsp) olive oil
4–5 shallots
4 ripe tomatoes
250g (9oz) minced meat
2 stalks of celery
150ml ($\frac{1}{4}$pt) dry red wine
parsley, cress (optional)
marjoram, basil
100g ($\frac{1}{4}$lb) cheese

1 Wash aubergines, remove stalks and cut into 3–4cm (1–1$\frac{1}{2}$in) thick slices. Sprinkle with coarse salt and leave in a cool place for 10 min.
2 Sauté chopped shallots in 1 × 15ml tbsp (1tbsp) oil, add minced meat and fork apart on strong heat until meat looks like breadcrumbs.
3 Scald and skin tomatoes and mix with finely cut celery, meat, red wine, seasonings and herbs.
4 Spoon mixture into an ovenproof dish and place dried aubergine slices on top. Brush these with remaining oil and place dish in oven. Place cheese slices on top for the last 6–8 min of cooking time.
Serve hot with bread or salad.

Above: Stuffed Tomatoes. Below: French Tomato Casserole.

Tomatoes and Peppers

Add a taste of summer to your cooking with ripe, juicy tomatoes and crisp peppers. Packed with Vitamin C, they're good for you too.

Tomatoes are expensive out of season, but canned ones provide a tasty and cheap alternative.

Fresh peppers (capsicums) may be red, green or yellow. They are delicious when stuffed, and when raw and cut into strips add colour and crispness to a summer salad.

Stuffed Peppers (right)
(serves 4)
Preparation time: 20 min
Cooking time: about 25 min
Oven temperature: 200°C, 400°F, Gas 6
Middle part of the oven
Unsuitable for the freezer

4 large green or red peppers
butter
100ml (4fl oz) stock or tomato juice
Stuffing: see Stuffed Tomatoes

1 Wash and deseed peppers. Cut off tops for lids. Boil for 5 min in lightly salted water.
2 Drain well and stuff with meat or rice stuffing. Place lids on.
3 Place peppers in a greased, oven-proof dish with stock or tomato juice poured round. Brush with melted butter and bake in oven until tender.

Stuffed Tomatoes
(serves 4)
Preparation time: 15 min
Cooking time: about 40 min
Oven tempeature: 200–220°C, 400–425°F, Gas 6–7
Middle part of the oven
Unsuitable for the freezer

8 large tomatoes
salt, pepper
2 onions
250g (9oz) minced beef
½–1 garlic clove
40g (1½oz) butter
2–3 × 15ml tbsp (2–3tbsp) stock
parsley
breadcrumbs or grated cheese

1 Wash tomatoes, cut off tops and remove cores and pulp with a spoon. Sprinkle with a little salt and turn upside down.

2 Sauté coarsely chopped onions, minced beef and garlic in half the butter, forking up mixture until it resembles breadcrumbs. Add stock, seasoning and finely chopped parsley and simmer until meat is cooked.

3 Divide stuffing between tomatoes and place in a greased, ovenproof dish. Sprinkle with breadcrumbs or grated cheese and dot on remaining butter. Bake as directed for 10–15 min.
Serve with bread and a salad.

VARIATION (below right)
Tomatoes Stuffed with Rice
Use minced pork instead of beef. Sauté 100g ($\frac{1}{4}$lb) chopped mushrooms in a little butter. Mix 50g (2oz) cooked rice, 2–3 × 15ml tbsp (2–3tbsp) tomato purée, 1 egg, 1 × 15ml tbsp (1tbsp) fresh or 1 × 5ml tsp (1tsp) dried basil, salt and pepper.

French Tomato Casserole
(serves 4–5)
Preparation time: 1 hr
Cooking time: 15–20 min
Suitable for the freezer, but will lose some flavour

$\frac{1}{2}$–$\frac{3}{4}$kg ($1\frac{1}{4}$–$1\frac{1}{2}$lb) ripe tomatoes
2 small courgettes
salt, 1 small aubergine
2–3 onions
50g (2oz) bacon
paprika
1–2 garlic cloves
pepper, 10 olives
100ml (4fl oz) dry red wine
parsley, thyme, majoram, basil

1 Wash vegetables and cut into slices or strips. Scald and peel tomatoes before slicing them. Sprinkle coarse salt on sliced aubergine and courgettes and leave in a cool place for about $\frac{1}{2}$ hr.

2 Sauté sliced onion and bacon in small cubes on moderate heat. Add crushed garlic, dried aubergine and courgettes, tomatoes, olives and red wine. Simmer for 10 min. Add finely chopped herbs and simmer for a further 5–10 min. Season with salt, pepper and paprika. Serve with fried or grilled meats.

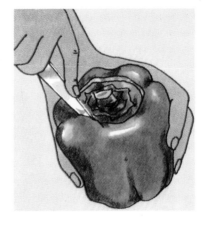
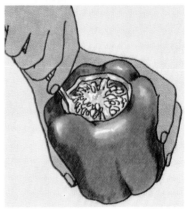

To Deseed Peppers
1 Wash and dry pepper. Cut round stalk and pull out. The core will loosen and most of the seeds will come out.

2 Scrape out the rest of the core with a spoon and rinse pepper in cold water. Cut into strips, cubes or stuff whole.

Fennel

This is an unusual vegetable, rather like celery to look at. Although not yet used by many housewives it is available in the supermarkets.

Fennel has a bulbous, white root, light-green stalks and feathery green leaves. It has a sweet flavour not unlike aniseed.

The bulbous part is used for cooking. The stalks can be used raw – thinly sliced in salads or whole with cheese – or cooked. The light-green top is finely chopped and used as a herb.

Fennel with Ham and Cheese

1 Rinse fennel and cut off root base, top and stalks. Slice stalks and use with roots.

2 Slice roots and place in boiling, lightly salted water, with a little lemon juice added. Simmer until barely tender. Remove with a slotted spoon and place on a plate or in a colander.

3 Place well-drained fennel roots in a greased, ovenproof dish with ham cubes in between.

4 Sprinkle with a thin layer of grated cheese and dot with melted butter. Place dish in preheated oven, with high upper heat. Cheese is also used for the sauce (see recipe).

Fennel with Ham and Cheese is a nourishing dinner dish which does not take all that long to prepare. Serve with boiled potatoes generously sprinkled with parsley.

Fennel with Ham and Cheese

(serves 4)
Preparation time: 20 min
Cooking time: 30 min
Oven temperature: 220°C, 425°F, Gas 7
Suitable for the freezer, but will lose some flavour

2 large fennel
salt, ½ lemon
100g (¼lb) grated cheese
150–200g (5–7oz) cooked ham
40g (1½oz) butter
1–1½ × 15ml tbsp (1–1½tbsp) flour
1 egg yolk
200ml (7fl oz) cream
white pepper, nutmeg

1 Boil fennel for 15 min as directed in illustrations, but save stock. Place in a greased, ovenproof dish with the ham cubes. Sprinkle with 2–3 × 15ml tbsp (2–3tbsp) grated cheese and dot with 2 × 15ml tbsp (2tbsp) melted butter. Bake as directed for 15 min.
2 Melt remaining butter, stir in flour, but do not allow to brown. Add 200–300ml (7–10fl oz) fennel stock and boil until smooth, stirring continuously. Stir egg yolk with cream and add to sauce. Stir in remaining cheese.
Keep sauce just below boiling point until cheese has melted. Season with salt, pepper and nutmeg. Sprinkle dish with finely chopped fennel top and serve with sauce and boiled potatoes generously sprinkled with parsley.

Fried Fennel with Tomato

(serves 4)
Preparation time: 15 min
Cooking time: 15–20 min
Suitable for the freezer, but will lose some flavour

2 fennel
50g (2oz) chopped bacon
15g (½oz) butter
1 onion, ½ lemon
salt, pepper
1 small can of tomatoes
½ × 5ml tsp (½tsp) dried mixed herbs

1 Cut off green leaves and root base and rinse fennel well. Cut into four lengthways, cut root part once more, to avoid their being too thick compared with stalks.
2 Gently heat bacon in a frying pan until fat escapes. Add the butter and fry fennel and sliced onion in the fats.
3 Lower heat and add juice from ½ lemon, salt, pepper, tomatoes with their juice and dried herbs. Simmer, covered, until fennel is tender. Sprinkle with finely chopped fennel tops. Serve with fried fish, mutton, beef or poultry.

VARIATION
Add pieces of meat, meat balls or small sausages to the dish when nearly done. Transfer to an ovenproof dish, sprinkle generously with grated cheese and bake for 15–20 min at 200–220°C, 400–425°F, Gas 6–7 until everything is tender and cheese golden.
Serve with bread and butter and a green salad.

Globe Artichokes and Corn-on-the-Cob

The thistle-like artichoke and the yellow corn cob are most unusual vegetables in appearance, and their taste is just as interesting.

Artichokes are boiled and served hot with softened butter, or cold with an oil and vinegar marinade. It is the thick, bottom part of the leaves and the pale-green heart which we eat. Corn-on-the-cob with a golden-yellow colour is the best. Yellow-white cobs are not ripe and the dark-yellow ones are too ripe. Whole cobs are boiled in lightly salted water and served with chilled butter. They are very good grilled.

Stuffed Artichokes (left)
(serves 4)
Preparation time: 15 min
Cooking time: 40–50 min
Unsuitable for the freezer

4 large artichokes
salt, pepper
150–200g (5–7oz) mushrooms
butter
100–200g (4–7oz) cooked ham
2 hardboiled eggs
lemon juice
4 × 15ml tbsp (4tbsp) parsley or
  chives
150ml ($\frac{1}{4}$pt) dry white wine

To Clean Artichokes

1 Cut or break off the stalk on the artichoke.

2 Tear off the bottom coarse leaves. Cut off sharp leaf points with scissors.

3 Cut off the top part and remove some of the inner leaves.

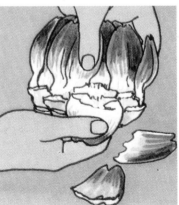

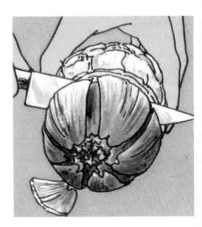

1 Cut off stem of artichokes and also the whole top section. Cut off sharp leaf tips. Rinse artichokes well in several cold waters and boil for 20–30 min in lightly salted water with a little lemon juice added.

2 Pull the inner leaves out carefully and remove fuzzy choke.

3 Sauté sliced mushrooms for a couple of min in 1 × 15ml tbsp (1tbsp) melted butter. Mix in ham cubes, chopped eggs, salt and pepper, lemon juice to taste and finely chopped parsley or chives.

4 Divide mixture between artichokes and place them in a deep pan. Pour in white wine and spoon a little melted butter over the filling.

Steam artichokes for 15–20 min on low heat.

Serve warm with French bread.

Deep-fried Corn (right)

Mix together 2 egg yolks, 100g ($\frac{1}{4}$lb) flour, 150ml ($\frac{1}{4}$pt) milk or water, 1 × 5ml tsp (1tsp) salt, 2 × 15ml tbsp (2tbsp) oil and 1 stiffly whisked egg white. Stir in 300–400g (11–14oz) corn kernels.

Place a spoonful of mixture in hot oil or lard and fry until lightly golden. Remove with slotted spoon and place on kitchen paper. Sprinkle with paprika as soon as mixture is ready.

Serve warm with poultry or other white meat.

When you only want to use the kernels, remove them with a sharp knife.

63

Index